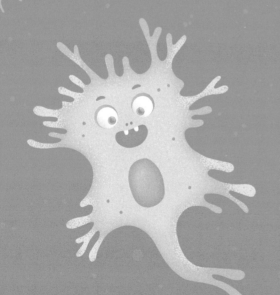

The Brain Book

Written by
Dr. Liam Drew

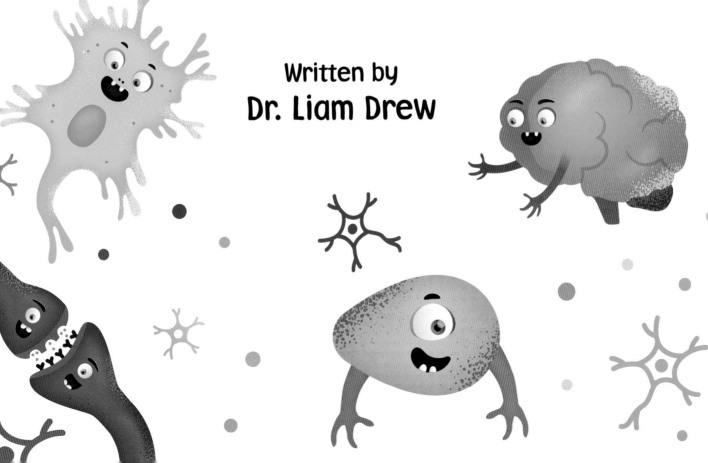

Contents

 Penguin Random House

Written by Dr. Liam Drew
Consultant Dr. Catherine Hall

Project Editor Olivia Stanford
Project Art Editors Polly Appleton, Lucy Sims
Illustrators Mark Clifton,
Bettina Myklebust Stovne
Additional Design Ann Cannings,
Sadie Thomas
US Senior Editor Shannon Beatty

US Editor Margaret Parrish
Jacket Coordinator Issy Walsh
Jacket Designer Bettina Myklebust Stovne
Production Editor Abi Maxwell
Senior Production Controller Inderjit Bhullar
Managing Editor Jonathan Melmoth
Managing Art Editor Diane Peyton Jones
Senior Picture Researcher Sumedha Chopra
Creative Director Helen Senior
Publishing Director Sarah Larter

First American Edition, 2021
Published in the United States by DK Publishing
1450 Broadway, Suite 801, New York, NY 10018

There are some **tricky words** used to describe the brain in this book! Check the **glossary** if you come across any you're not sure about.

A catalog record for this book
is available from the Library of Congress.
ISBN: 978-0-7440-2815-7

DK books are available at special discounts when
purchased in bulk for sales promotions, premiums,
fund-raising, or educational use. For details, contact:
DK Publishing Special Markets,
1450 Broadway, Suite 801, New York, NY 10018
SpecialSales@dk.com

Printed and bound in China

This book was made with Forest Stewardship Council ™
certified paper – one small step in DK's
commitment to a sustainable future.
For more information go to
www.dk.com/our-green-pledge

MIX
Paper from
responsible sources
FSC™ C018179

For the curious
www.dk.com

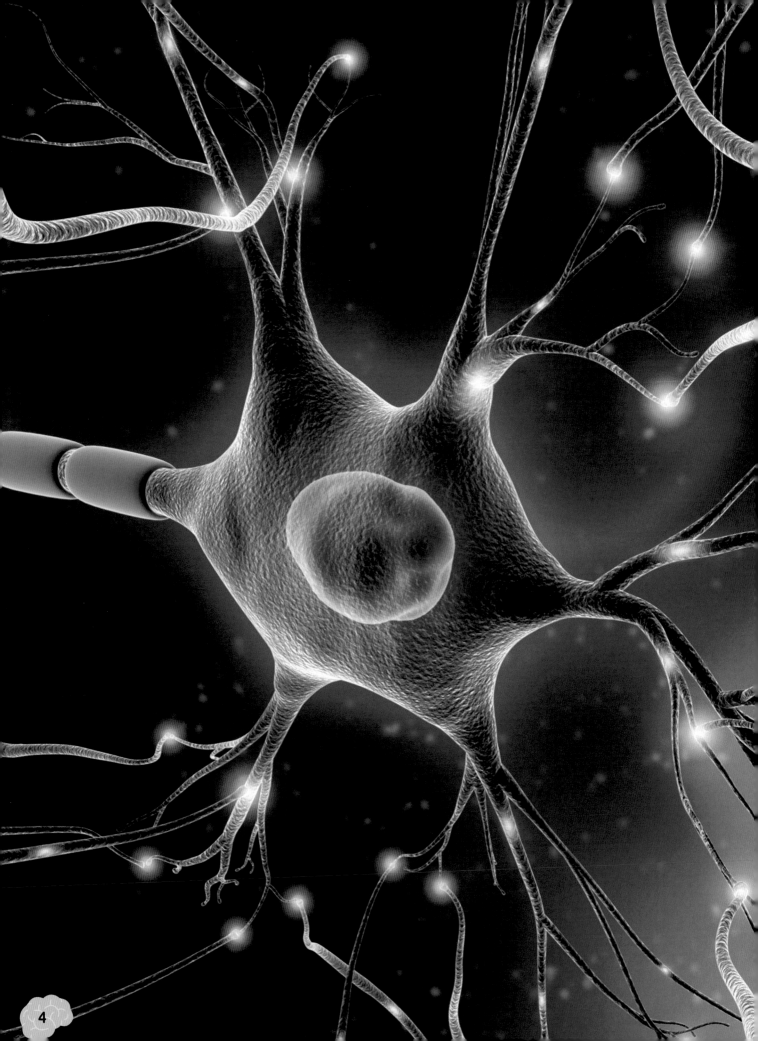

Introduction

This book is a voyage around the **inside of your head**. We're going to explore what brains are made of, how they work, and how they make you **who you are**. Everything that you feel, see, hear, taste, and smell depends on messages traveling around your brain. Every move you make is controlled by your brain and all your emotions—happiness and sadness, frustration and joy, fear and love—are **created by your brain**.

All brains are similar, but each one is **unique**. Some differences depend on information in the **DNA** we inherit from our parents, others are caused by our **experiences** and what we learn. Brains can absorb huge amounts of knowledge—I hope yours enjoys finding out about itself!

Liam Drew

Dr. Liam Drew

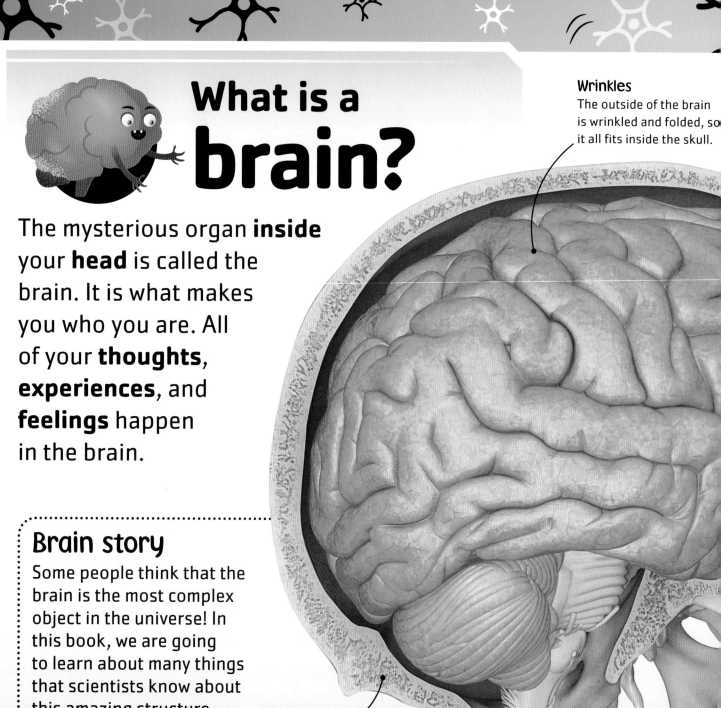

What is a brain?

The mysterious organ **inside** your **head** is called the brain. It is what makes you who you are. All of your **thoughts**, **experiences**, and **feelings** happen in the brain.

Brain story

Some people think that the brain is the most complex object in the universe! In this book, we are going to learn about many things that scientists know about this amazing structure.

Wrinkles
The outside of the brain is wrinkled and folded, so it all fits inside the skull.

Cranium
The largest part of the skull is a hard, bony case that protects the brain from physical damage.

Spinal cord
This carries messages to and from the brain and body.

WHY DO I NEED A BRAIN?

Your brain allows you to move around and do many things. It helps you to remember things, to learn, to eat and drink, to stay safe, and to make friends.

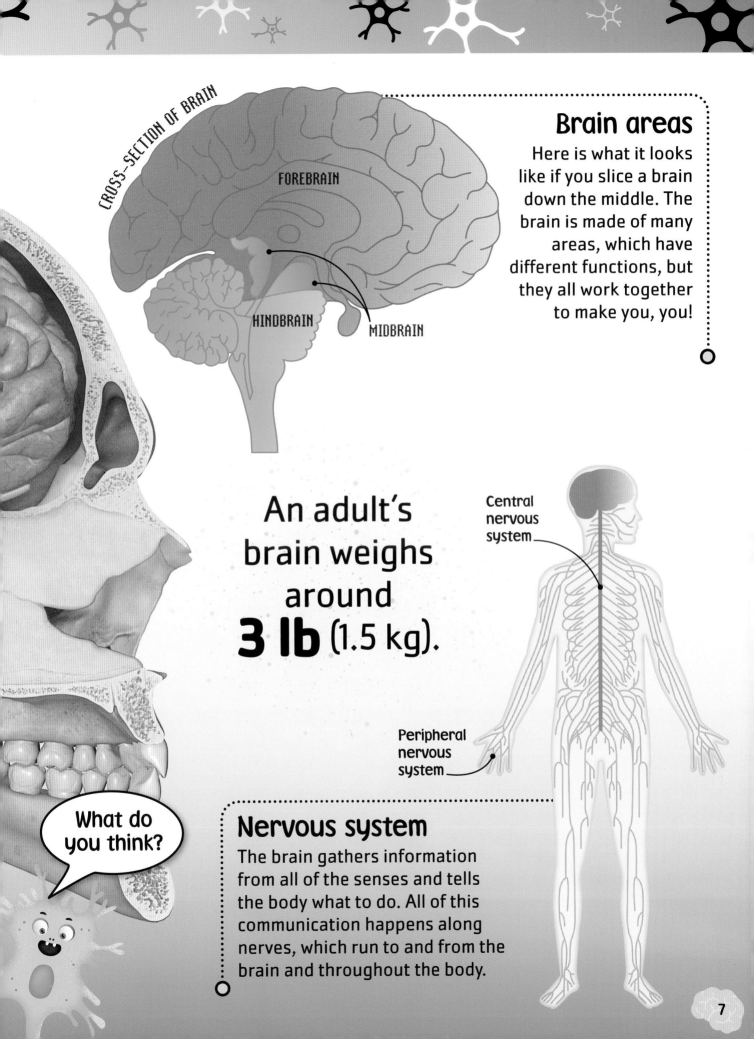

CROSS-SECTION OF BRAIN

FOREBRAIN

HINDBRAIN

MIDBRAIN

Brain areas

Here is what it looks like if you slice a brain down the middle. The brain is made of many areas, which have different functions, but they all work together to make you, you!

An adult's brain weighs around **3 lb** (1.5 kg).

Central nervous system

Peripheral nervous system

What do you think?

Nervous system

The brain gathers information from all of the senses and tells the body what to do. All of this communication happens along nerves, which run to and from the brain and throughout the body.

What does a
brain do?

The brain is the **control center** of your body. It **gathers information** about what's happening, **processes this information**, and then **controls how your body** responds. All brains work similarly, but the little differences make everyone unique.

Sight
The eyes take in visual information, such as a plane flying by outside.

Hunger
The brain gives you a feeling of hunger if you haven't eaten for a while.

That's a lot to do!

Gathering information

Your eyes, ears, and other sense organs turn information from the outside world into signals that are sent to the brain. The brain also keeps track of what's going on inside your body. It can tell you whether you're hungry, thirsty, sleepy, or in pain.

Controlling your body

All your muscles are controlled by the brain. By moving different muscles, the brain can make you run, jump up in the air, or grab a pen to write.

Hearing
Your ears sense noises, such as the school bell.

Processing information

When you think, your brain combines useful new information with useful stored information. You make memories of the most important things that you experience, think, and do.

Feelings
Your feelings, such as excitement when playing a sport, are produced by the brain.

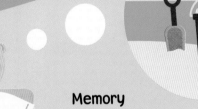

Memory
Your brain stores memories, such as a great beach vacation.

Thinking
Your brain does your thinking, such as solving a tough math problem.

Writing
The brain coordinates the delicate movements you need to be able to write.

Talking
The muscles you use to talk are under the brain's control.

Getting the body ready
Your heart—a big muscle—may pump a little faster if you're asked a question in class. This is because the brain prepares you for action.

9

Map of the brain

The brain is made up of **many parts**, each of which handles different **tasks**, such as understanding the words you read or the sounds you hear. Here's a **map** of the brain showing where these tasks happen.

Look in here!

Concentration, planning, and problem-solving

Movement control

FRONTAL LOBE

Speech

Smell

Body temperature, hunger, thirst, and many other body functions are controlled by the hypothalamus.

HYPOTHALAMUS

AMYGDALA

The amygdala controls our emotions and gives them meaning.

HIPPOCAMPUS

Memories are made in a long, thin structure called the hippocampus.

Looking inside

There are many more brain regions beneath the cerebral cortex, all of them with essential jobs. These include the limbic system, which controls our instincts, memories, and emotions.

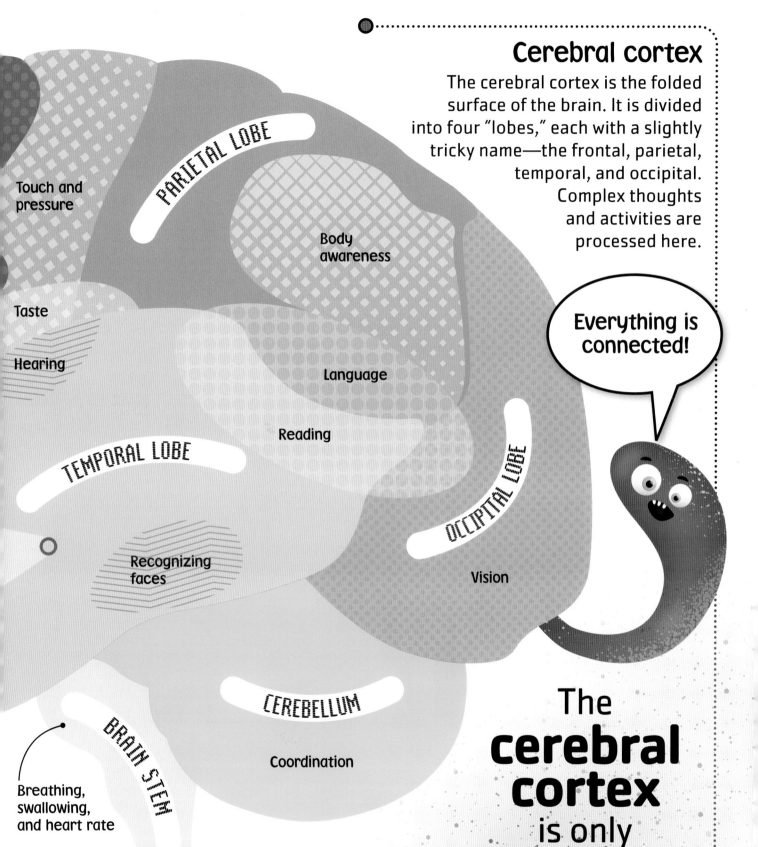

Cerebral cortex

The cerebral cortex is the folded surface of the brain. It is divided into four "lobes," each with a slightly tricky name—the frontal, parietal, temporal, and occipital. Complex thoughts and activities are processed here.

Everything is connected!

The **cerebral cortex** is only 0.1 in (2.5 mm) thick.

PARIETAL LOBE

Touch and pressure

Body awareness

Taste

Hearing

Language

Reading

TEMPORAL LOBE

OCCIPITAL LOBE

Recognizing faces

Vision

CEREBELLUM

Coordination

BRAIN STEM

Breathing, swallowing, and heart rate

Studying the **brain**

Scientists who study the brain are called **neuroscientists**. They do many different things to unlock the brain's **secrets**, including using brain scanners and microscopes and studying the effects of head injuries.

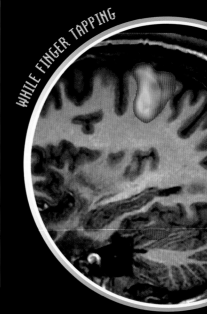

WHILE FINGER TAPPING

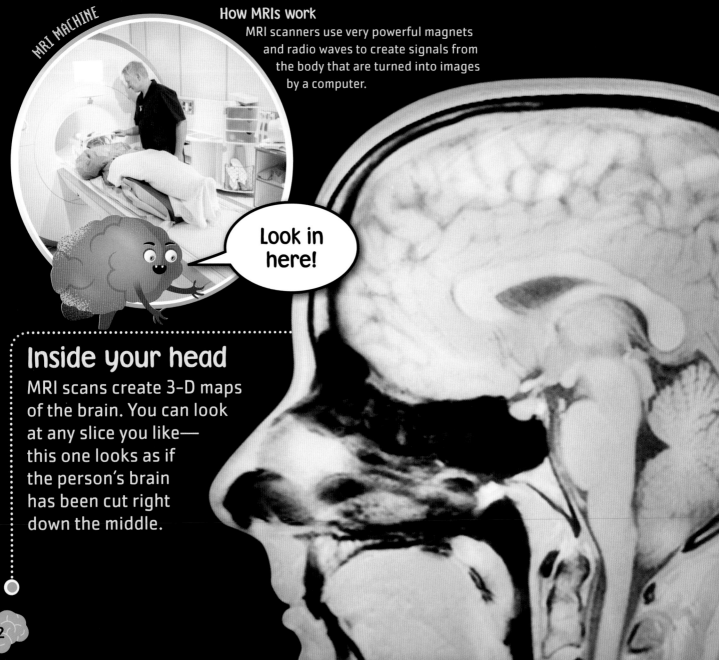

MRI MACHINE

How MRIs work
MRI scanners use very powerful magnets and radio waves to create signals from the body that are turned into images by a computer.

Look in here!

Inside your head

MRI scans create 3-D maps of the brain. You can look at any slice you like— this one looks as if the person's brain has been cut right down the middle.

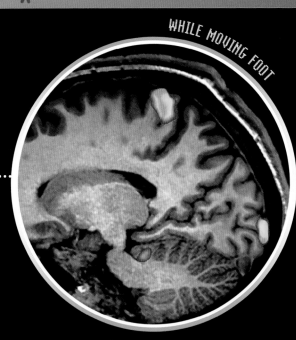

WHILE MOVING FOOT

The working brain

When a part of your brain becomes active, extra blood goes there. Scans can detect the oxygen in blood and therefore which brain regions are working when you do certain things.

NEURONS SHOWN IN GREEN

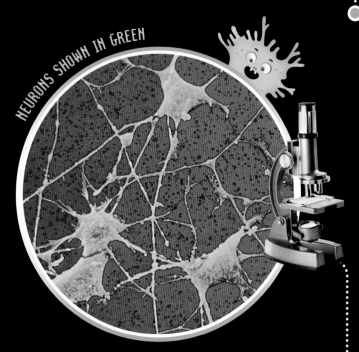

Neurons up-close

Scientists use microscopes to look at samples of the brain or neurons they grow in the lab. These help us understand how they work.

CASE STUDIES

If someone injures a part of their brain, it may change how their mind works. This can tell us what different brain regions do.

Music memory

If the hippocampus is damaged, people can lose the ability to form memories of new experiences. Older memories and learned skills are remembered, though.

Taking sides

Certain types of brain damage make people unable to see and respond to half of the world in front of them. They might only see half the food on a plate.

Who's that?

One part of the cerebral cortex responds to faces—damage to it leaves people unable to recognize anyone, even family and friends.

Amygdala

The amygdala helps control emotions, especially when somebody is feeling scared. It is found next to the hippocampus.

THE AMYGDALA

The amygdala is nestled inside the brain's limbic system.

Hippocampus

The hippocampus does one of the brain's most important jobs—it helps make memories. Let's look closer at what's inside...

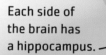

Each side of the brain has a hippocampus.

THE HIPPOCAMPUS

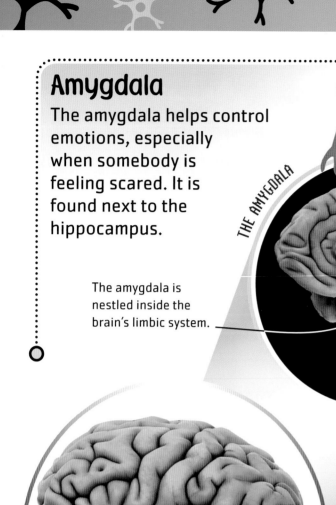

Brain

The brain is a very complex organ that contains many regions. Let's zoom in to see some of its parts...

Meet the mind

The closer **neuroscientists** look at the brain, the more they see. Here, we meet different parts of the brain. Knowing how each part works helps us **understand** the brain overall.

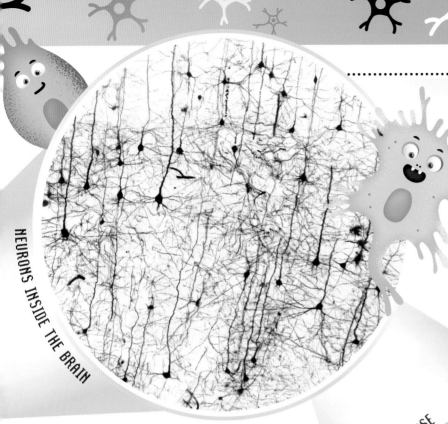

NEURONS INSIDE THE BRAIN

Neurons

If you look inside any part of the brain, you'll find it's full of neurons. These are wiry cells that are connected to each other, to pass messages among themselves.

SYNAPSE

Spikes

Spikes are not actual physical structures. They are little pulses of electricity that move along neurons to tell synapses when to send messages.

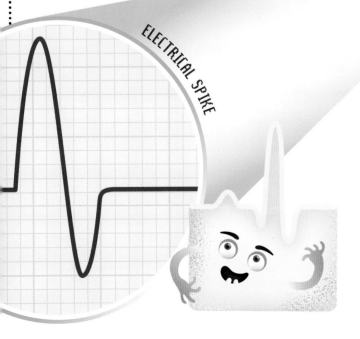

ELECTRICAL SPIKE

Synapses

If you look even closer at where neurons join each other, you'll find synapses. These structures use chemicals to relay information from one neuron to the next.

What is your brain made of?

To understand **how brains work**, we need to know what's **inside** them. A brain contains many brain cells and also lots of blood vessels to support them.

Feeding the brain

The brain uses more energy than any other body part, so it needs lots of blood to bring it food and oxygen. Laid out end to end, the brain's blood vessels would measure about 400 miles (645 km)!

Blood vessels
A branching network of blood vessels brings blood to the brain.

Why is it pink and squishy?

Brains feel like jelly because their cells contain lots of fat and there are no bones inside. Brain cells are cream-colored, which combined with all the blood makes brains look pink.

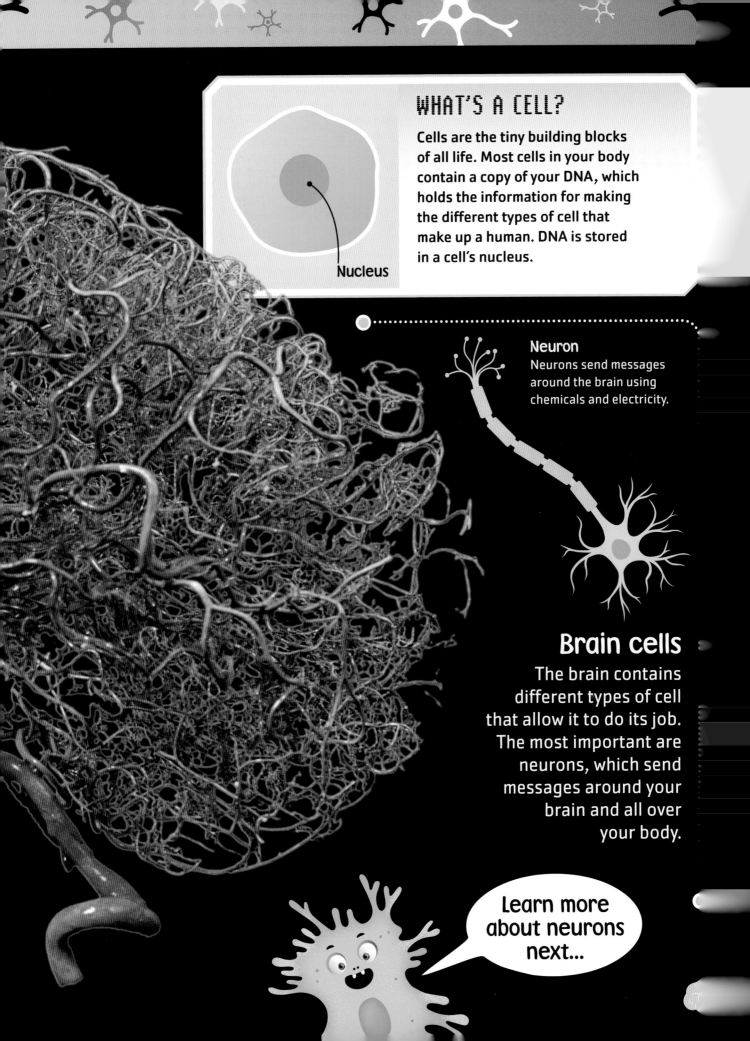

WHAT'S A CELL?

Cells are the tiny building blocks of all life. Most cells in your body contain a copy of your DNA, which holds the information for making the different types of cell that make up a human. DNA is stored in a cell's nucleus.

Nucleus

Neuron
Neurons send messages around the brain using chemicals and electricity.

Brain cells

The brain contains different types of cell that allow it to do its job. The most important are neurons, which send messages around your brain and all over your body.

Learn more about neurons next...

Making connections

The cells that carry **messages** around your brain—making you think, feel, sense, and act— are called **neurons**. A human brain contains roughly **86 billion** neurons and 84 billion other cells!

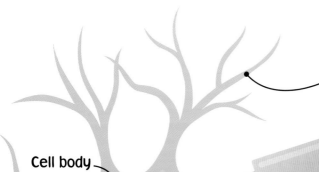

Dendrites
Around their cell body, neurons have branches—called dendrites—that collect incoming messages.

Cell body

Nucleus

Axon
Each neuron has a long, wiry axon, which it uses to send outgoing messages.

Myelin sheath
Most axons are wrapped in a fatty substance called myelin, which makes messages travel faster.

The longest **axon** in your body runs from your big toe to the base of your **brain**!

Neurons

The brain and nerves in your body contain neurons. Neurons connect to each other to create a network that information travels around. Each neuron collects incoming messages, then sends messages to other neurons or body parts.

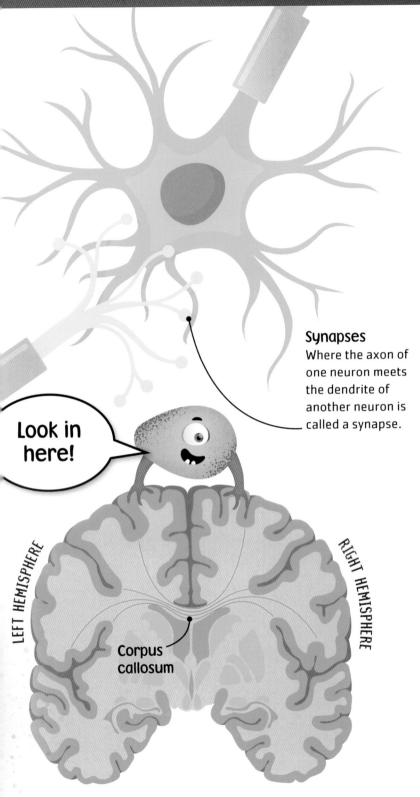

Synapses
Where the axon of one neuron meets the dendrite of another neuron is called a synapse.

Look in here!

LEFT HEMISPHERE

RIGHT HEMISPHERE

Corpus callosum

Connecting the brain
The right and left sides, or hemispheres, of the brain are actually separate structures. Large bundles of axons connect one side to the other. The largest bundle is called the corpus callosum.

Supporting cells
Neurons might be the most important brain cells, but the brain couldn't function without other types of cell, too. Find out about some of these below.

Oligodendrocytes
These are fatty cells that wrap around axons in the brain to make the myelin sheaths.

Microglia
Microglia fight any germs that get into the brain and remove broken pieces of cells.

Astrocytes
Astrocytes create the brain's structure, supply nutrients, and repair damage.

Pericytes
These cells control blood flow and decide what leaves the blood to enter the brain.

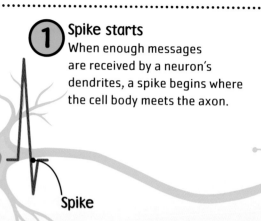

Spike starts

(1) When enough messages are received by a neuron's dendrites, a spike begins where the cell body meets the axon.

Spike

Spike travels

(2) The electrical spike then travels down the axon, away from the cell body toward the synapses.

Spikes

Information travels through neurons by electrical impulses, called spikes. The number and pattern of spikes carries the information—about incoming sensory signals, memories and feelings, or outgoing instructions to control the body.

Sending impulses

Neurons carry **information** around the brain and the rest of the nervous system using two things: tiny **electrical** and **chemical** messages. Even your thoughts are carried by electrical impulses!

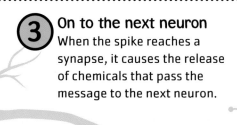

3 On to the next neuron
When the spike reaches a synapse, it causes the release of chemicals that pass the message to the next neuron.

Spikes travel down axons without myelin, a little like a **wave** moving across the sea.

WHITE AND GRAY MATTER

Some neurons are wrapped in a fatty myelin sheath. This helps speed up electrical spikes. Neurons with a myelin sheath look white, and neurons without one look gray.

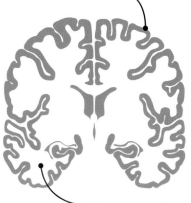

The cerebral cortex is made of gray matter

The center of the brain is made of white matter

Weak signal
The fewer messages a neuron receives telling it to spike, the fewer spikes it sends.

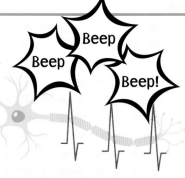

Strong signal
When lots of messages arrive at a neuron's dendrites, it fires lots of spikes.

INCREASING THE SIGNAL

Imagine a neuron that tracks how hungry you are—if you're full, it doesn't make any spikes, but as your stomach empties, the more spikes it creates. More spikes make you feel hungrier.

Crossing the divide

When a spike reaches the end of an axon, it causes the release of chemical messengers called **neurotransmitters** at a tiny structure known as a **synapse**. The chemicals pass on the message to the next neuron.

Most brain neurons form synapses with thousands of other neurons.

Synapses

Synapses link neurons together. They contain the end of one neuron's axon, a tiny gap, and part of the dendrite of the next neuron. Chemical messages cross the gap in about one thousandth of a second!

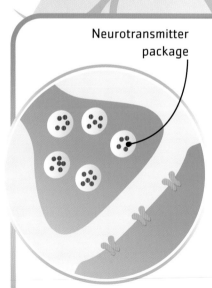

Neurotransmitter package

Ready to go
Neurotransmitters are stored in little round packages in an axon's end. When a neuron is quiet, they remain still but ready to move.

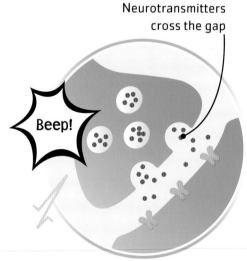

Neurotransmitters cross the gap

Beep!

Neurotransmitter release
An electrical spike causes some packages to move to the edge of the neuron and release the neurotransmitters inside into the gap.

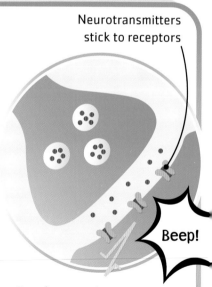

Neurotransmitters stick to receptors

Beep!

Passing on the message
The neurotransmitters spread to the next neuron and stick to receptors there, which change that neuron's electrical activity and can cause it to spike.

Stop or go?

There are two types of synapse: inhibitory (STOP) and excitatory (GO). STOP synapses make it less likely that the next neuron will spike. GO synapses do the opposite. Neurons add up all the STOP and GO signals they receive to decide whether to spike.

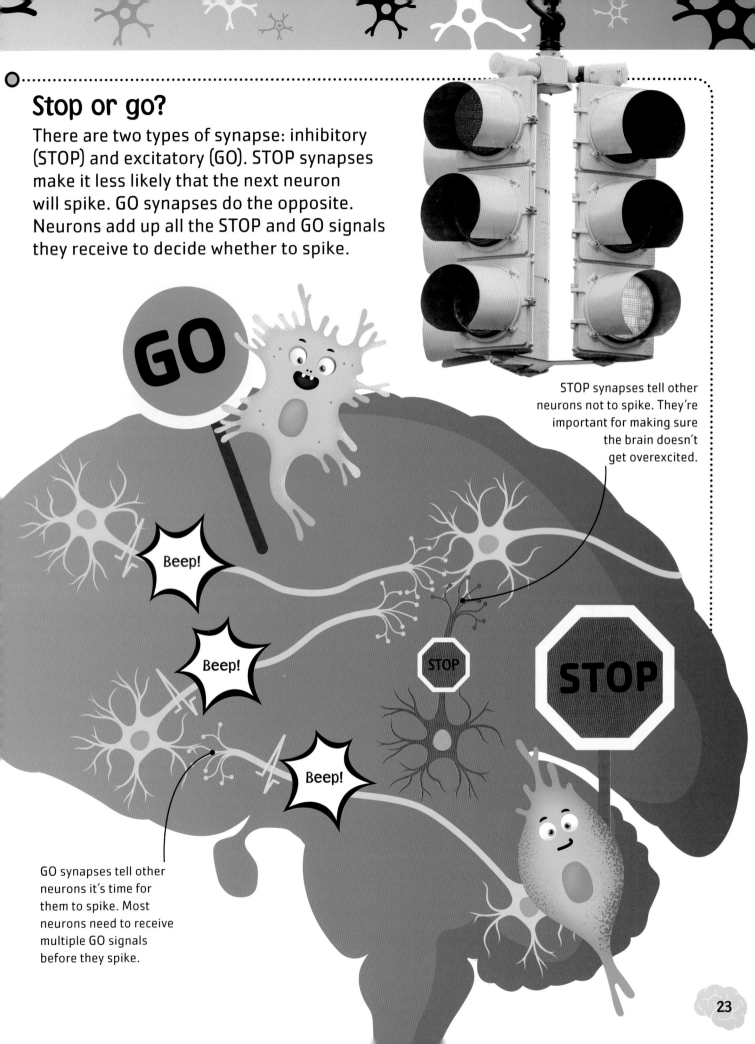

STOP synapses tell other neurons not to spike. They're important for making sure the brain doesn't get overexcited.

GO

Beep!

Beep!

Beep!

STOP

STOP

GO synapses tell other neurons it's time for them to spike. Most neurons need to receive multiple GO signals before they spike.

Reflexes

Reflexes are automatic responses to a particular event—for example, sneezing when something irritates the nose. All animals have reflexes, and the brain isn't always involved in them. Spikes can travel directly from sensory organs to the spinal cord, then straight back to the muscles to cause a response.

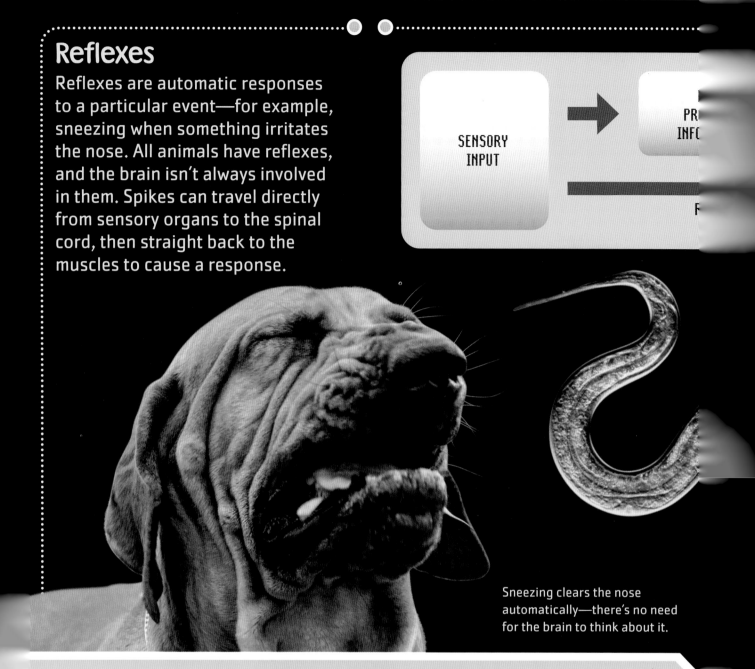

SENSORY
INPUT

PR
INF

F

Sneezing clears the nose automatically—there's no need for the brain to think about it.

Basic brains

Human brains are very **complicated**, so many neuroscientists study animals with much **simpler** brains. This allows them to figure out the **basic ways** in which brains work, which helps us to understand all brains.

Reflexes vs. thinking

The brain and nervous system use information to help an animal survive. The simplest brains mainly use reflexes. Thinking is slower, as new sensory information is mixed with an animal's knowledge and thoughts about what it needs, before an action is chosen. The more complex a brain is, the more thinking it does.

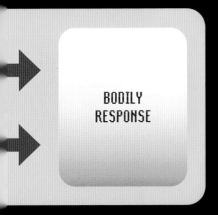

BODILY RESPONSE

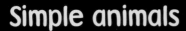

C. elegans uses mainly reflexes. If you touch either end of it, it automatically slithers away in the opposite direction.

NEURONS ARE SHOWN IN BLUE AND GREEN. MUSCLES ARE SHOWN IN RED.

Simple animals

Some neuroscientists study a tiny worm called C. elegans. All 302 of the worm's neurons have been identified and scientists can now watch how messages travel between all the neurons to explain the worm's simple behavior.

Not all animals have brains.

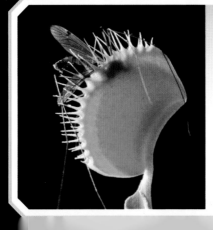

PLANTS VS. ANIMALS

Animals need brains because they move around. Plants live their lives in one place, so they don't need brains—although some, such as the Venus flytrap, have developed ways of moving quickly without neurons!

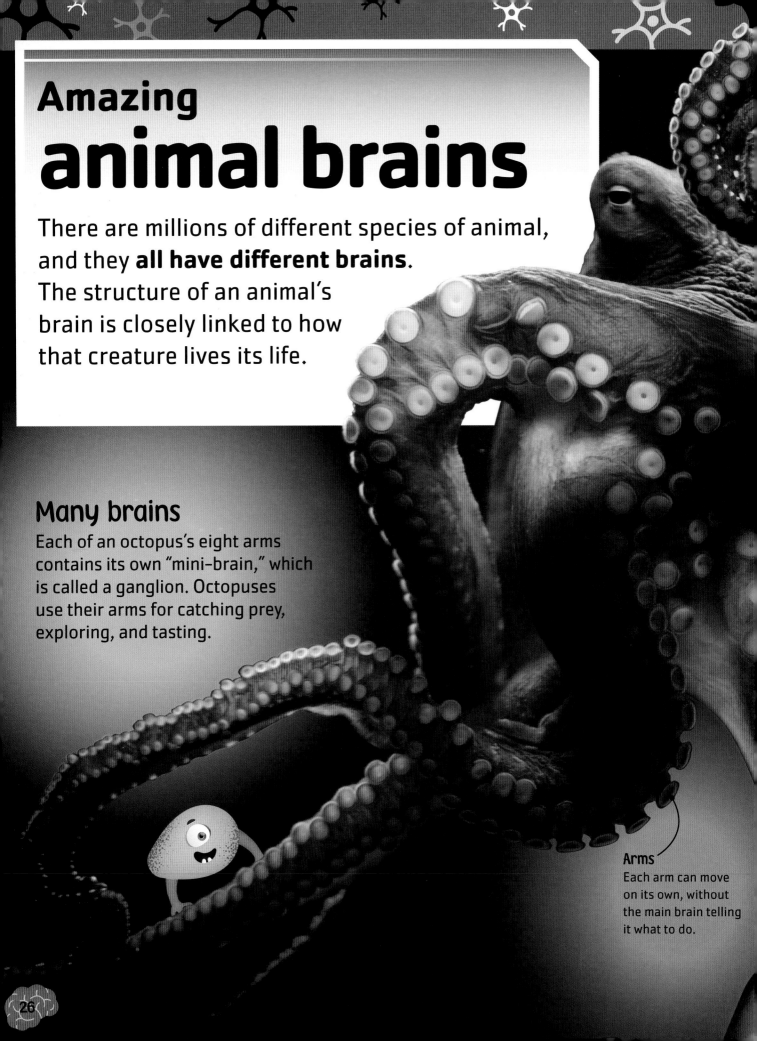

Amazing
animal brains

There are millions of different species of animal, and they **all have different brains**. The structure of an animal's brain is closely linked to how that creature lives its life.

Many brains

Each of an octopus's eight arms contains its own "mini-brain," which is called a ganglion. Octopuses use their arms for catching prey, exploring, and tasting.

Arms
Each arm can move on its own, without the main brain telling it what to do.

The octopus
is the most
intelligent
animal without
a backbone.

Shrinking shrews
In winter, food is scarce, so the common shrew shrinks its brain and skull to save energy. In spring, the brain grows back!

Walking brains
Tiny spiders have fairly big brains to help them build webs. In some species, the brain takes up 80 percent of the body and even spills into the legs!

No-brainers
Sea squirts have disappearing brains! Baby sea squirts can swim, but adult sea squirts stick to rocks, so they don't need a brain. As they grow, they absorb it.

Evolution

Humans belong to the ape family. By studying fossils of other species of human that no longer exist, we can see how modern humans evolved. Fossil skulls tell us how their brains changed in size and shape.

MYA = Million Years Ago
BCE = Before Common Era

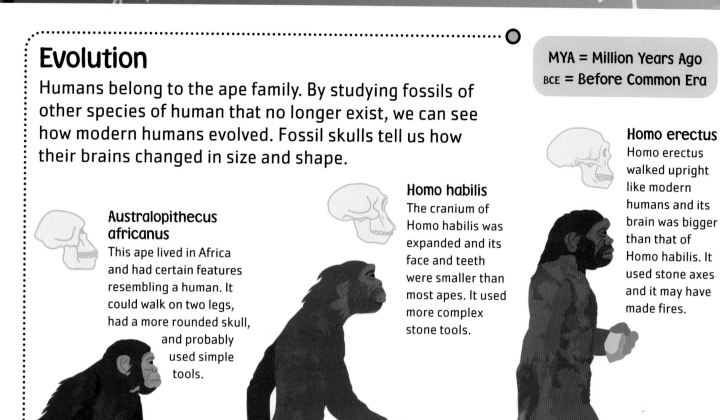

Homo erectus

Homo erectus walked upright like modern humans and its brain was bigger than that of Homo habilis. It used stone axes and it may have made fires.

Homo habilis

The cranium of Homo habilis was expanded and its face and teeth were smaller than most apes. It used more complex stone tools.

Australopithecus africanus

This ape lived in Africa and had certain features resembling a human. It could walk on two legs, had a more rounded skull, and probably used simple tools.

3.3-2.1 MYA

2.4-1.6 MYA

1.8 MYA-100,000 BCE

Becoming human

To understand where humans came from, scientists look at **fossils** and closely related animals. One of the most important parts of human **evolution** was the brain getting **bigger**.

Homo neanderthalensis

Neanderthals were modern humans' closest relatives. They were shorter and more muscular, but their brains were the same size. They wore primitive clothes.

Homo sapiens

Our species evolved around 300,000 years ago. Our brains have not changed much since then, but human lifestyles are different because of what we've learned.

300,000 BCE–present

400,000–40,000 BCE

Close cousins

Chimpanzees are our closest living relatives—99% of their DNA is the same as ours! Their brain is three times smaller than a human's, but they make and use simple tools.

Family tree

Evolution doesn't happen in a straight line. Many types of human species branched off from our ape ancestors, but only one branch led to modern humans.

Australopithecus

Homo habilis

Homo erectus

Homo neanderthalensis

Homo sapiens

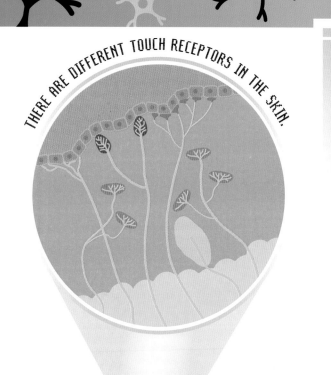

Feeling
touch

All over the **surface** of your body are tiny **receptors** that sense when something comes into **contact** with your skin. Touch, temperature, and pain are sensed by different receptors

Touch axons
Long axons run from your fingertips along touch neurons to the spinal cord.

Skin senses

Touch-sensing neurons connect to receptor cells that detect touch and pressure. Other neurons, unconnected to these cells, sense touch, temperature, itching, and pain.

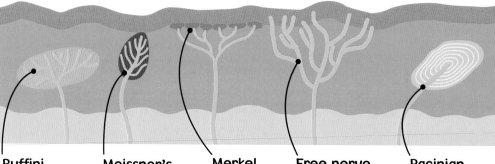

Ruffini ending
This receptor cell responds to the skin stretching.

Meissner's corpuscle
Very gentle touch signals are detected by this receptor cell.

Merkel cell
This touch receptor helps feel light touch.

Free nerve ending
Axons in the skin respond to pain, itching, and temperature.

Pacinian corpuscle
This cell type detects sudden touch and vibrations.

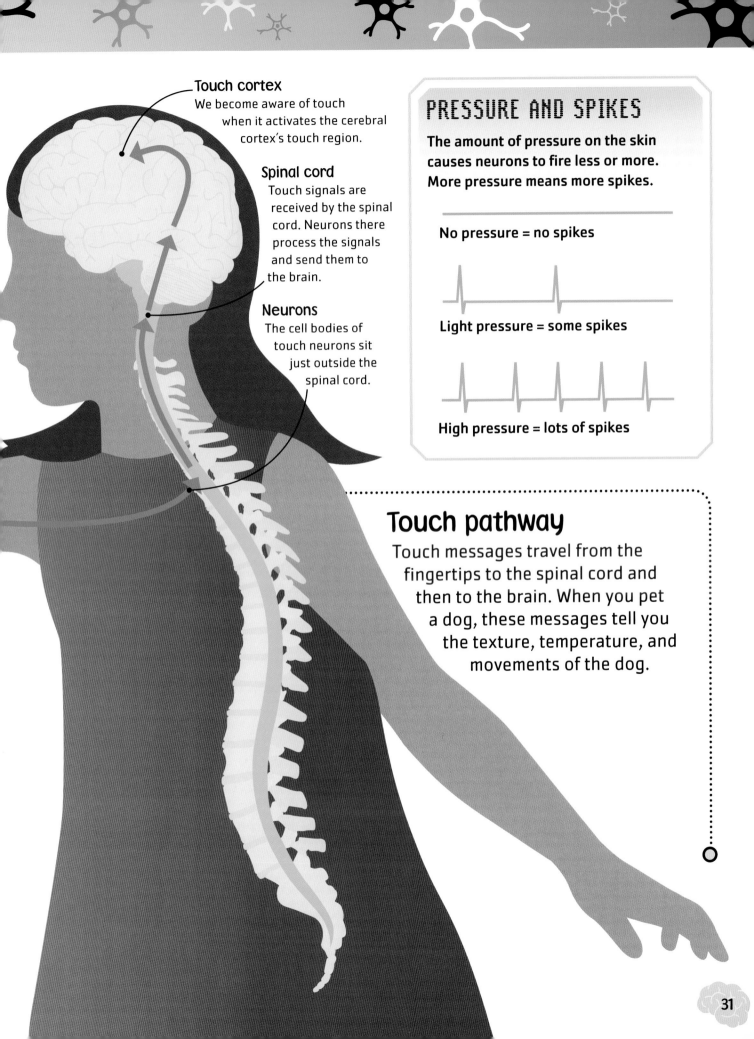

Touch cortex
We become aware of touch when it activates the cerebral cortex's touch region.

Spinal cord
Touch signals are received by the spinal cord. Neurons there process the signals and send them to the brain.

Neurons
The cell bodies of touch neurons sit just outside the spinal cord.

PRESSURE AND SPIKES

The amount of pressure on the skin causes neurons to fire less or more. More pressure means more spikes.

No pressure = no spikes

Light pressure = some spikes

High pressure = lots of spikes

Touch pathway

Touch messages travel from the fingertips to the spinal cord and then to the brain. When you pet a dog, these messages tell you the texture, temperature, and movements of the dog.

Strawberry smell

Things smell if they release chemicals into the air. The nose contains many different neurons with receptors for different airborne chemicals. The mix of chemicals that creates a smell activates only some of these neurons.

YOUR NOSE CONTAINS 400 DIFFERENT SMELL RECEPTORS.

SMELL RECEPTOR 1

SMELL RECEPTOR 2

SMELL RECEPTOR 3

SMELL RECEPTOR 4

SMELL RECEPTOR 5

Beep!

Elephants have the most smell receptors of any animal—more than **2,000**!

Memory lane

The path that smell information takes into the brain connects to regions that deal with memory and emotion. That's why many people have strong memories associated with smells, which are brought back by sniffing the familiar scent.

Smell and taste

Smell and taste are triggered by **chemicals**. If you breathe certain chemicals in the air into your **nose**, you smell them. Chemicals in food can activate taste buds on your **tongue**.

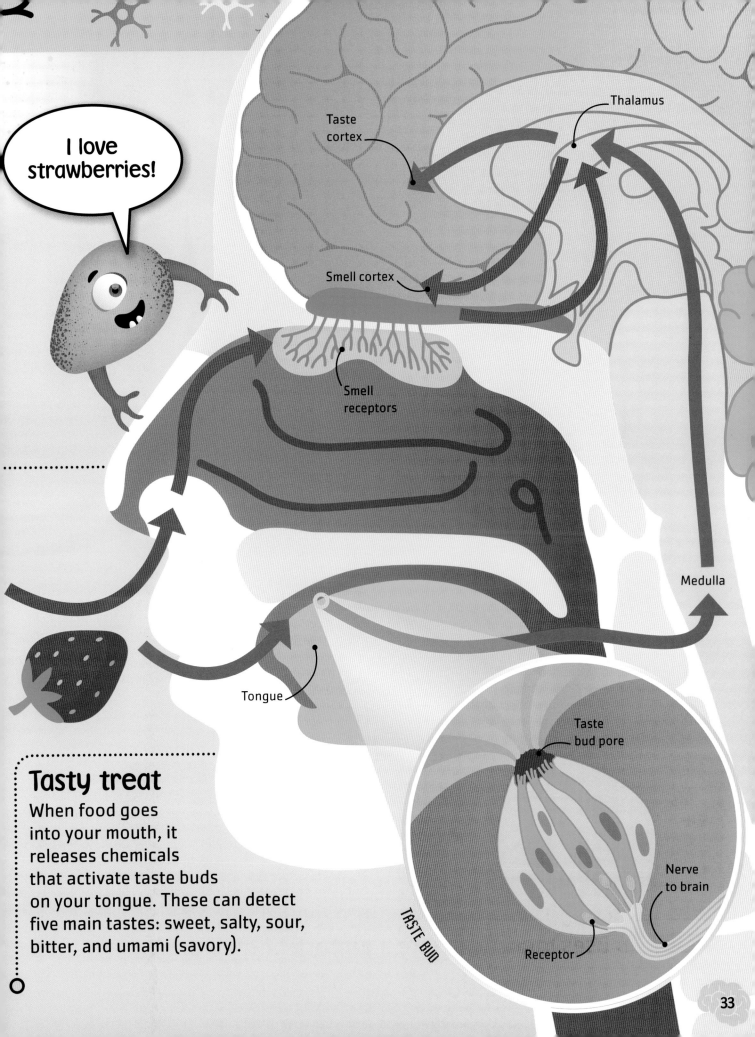

I love strawberries!

Thalamus

Taste cortex

Smell cortex

Smell receptors

Medulla

Tongue

Taste bud pore

Nerve to brain

Receptor

TASTE BUD

Tasty treat
When food goes into your mouth, it releases chemicals that activate taste buds on your tongue. These can detect five main tastes: sweet, salty, sour, bitter, and umami (savory).

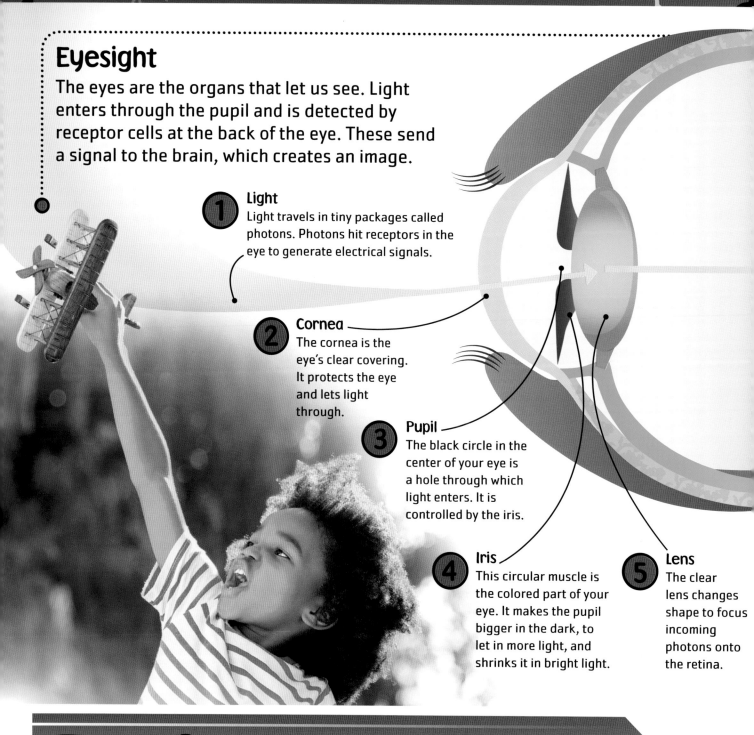

Eyesight

The eyes are the organs that let us see. Light enters through the pupil and is detected by receptor cells at the back of the eye. These send a signal to the brain, which creates an image.

1 **Light**
Light travels in tiny packages called photons. Photons hit receptors in the eye to generate electrical signals.

2 **Cornea**
The cornea is the eye's clear covering. It protects the eye and lets light through.

3 **Pupil**
The black circle in the center of your eye is a hole through which light enters. It is controlled by the iris.

4 **Iris**
This circular muscle is the colored part of your eye. It makes the pupil bigger in the dark, to let in more light, and shrinks it in bright light.

5 **Lens**
The clear lens changes shape to focus incoming photons onto the retina.

Seeing things

The sense of **vision** is very important to humans. The eyes gather **light** and convert it into neural signals. The brain uses these to create a **picture** of the world.

 Thalamus
The first stop for visual signals in the brain is the thalamus. From here, they are sent to the visual cortex.

 Visual cortex
The brain forms an internal image of the world when visual signals reach the visual cortex.

 Optic nerve
Signals from the retina are passed to neurons whose axons run to the brain.

 Retina
Receptors that detect photons to create electrical signals are found in a sheet, called the retina, at the back of the eye.

Making pictures

The visual cortex is divided into regions that look after different parts of vision. Some regions focus on color, for example, others movement, and some combine the two images taken by your left and right eye.

OPTICAL ILLUSION

The brain sometimes gets it wrong. The different colors and shapes in the image to the right trick the brain so that it sees movement. This is called an optical illusion.

Listening

Sound is detected by the ears. When sound vibrations travel into the ear they are turned into electrical signals by receptor cells, called hair cells. The brain turns these signals into sounds.

3 **Hammer, anvil, and stirrup**
In the air-filled middle part of the ear, there are three tiny bones that move when the eardrum vibrates.

2 **Eardrum**
This thin membrane vibrates when sound waves reach it.

1 **Sound waves**
Sound travels through the air as vibrations.

4 **Oval window**
The stirrup bone taps on the oval window, another membrane, to send vibrations into the fluid-filled inner ear, or cochlea.

5 **Cochlea**
The inner ear is spiral-shaped and contains hair cells that change vibrations into electrical signals.

Hearing sounds

Sounds, such as the singing of a bird, are vibrating **waves of air**. You detect them when they enter your ears. There, sounds are converted into signals that are sent to the **brain**.

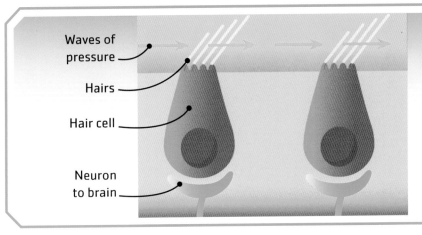

HAIR CELLS

Hair cells are found inside the cochlea. Each cell is topped with tiny hairlike structures that bend when vibrations pass through the fluid inside the cochlea. This bending generates electrical signals that are then sent to the brain.

Waves of pressure

Hairs

Hair cell

Neuron to brain

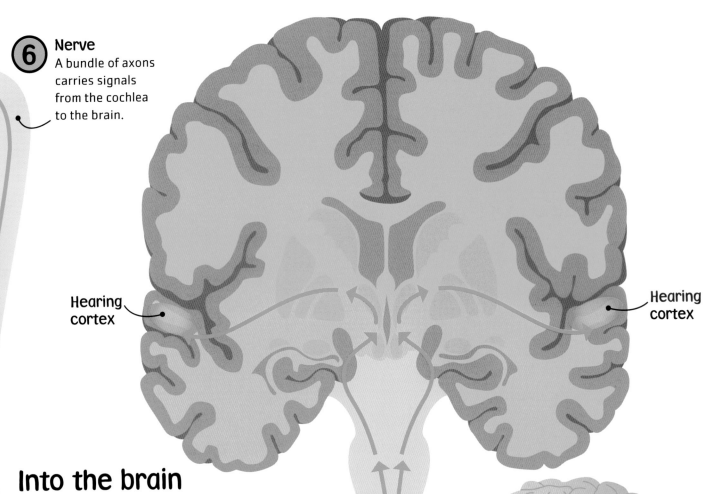

6 **Nerve**
A bundle of axons carries signals from the cochlea to the brain.

Hearing cortex

Hearing cortex

Into the brain

When sound messages enter the brain, it compares the timing of the signals from the right and left ears to determine the direction the sound came from.

Hearing cortex
You become aware of sounds when signals reach the hearing cortex on either side of the brain.

Making us move

We need to **move** to do all sorts of things: to search for food, escape danger, to play, or to exercise. The brain makes the body move by controlling its **muscles**.

Bend
When a signal is sent to contract your biceps, your arm bends.

Many muscles
This is what the body looks like beneath the skin! Most muscles are attached to bones. The body moves when these muscles pull on the bones to move the skeleton.

Straighten
When a signal is sent to contract your triceps, your arm straightens.

Bend or straighten
Muscles mainly come in pairs, such as the biceps and triceps in your arms. They are controlled by the nervous system. Signals from the brain tell a muscle to shorten—or contract—to make you move. If there is no signal, the muscle stays relaxed.

The human body contains roughly **700 muscles**.

MOVEMENT CORTEX

Three areas of the cerebral cortex help control movement. They work with structures inside the brain to make you move.

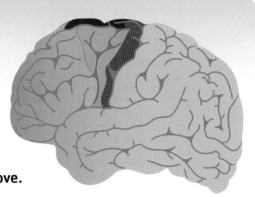

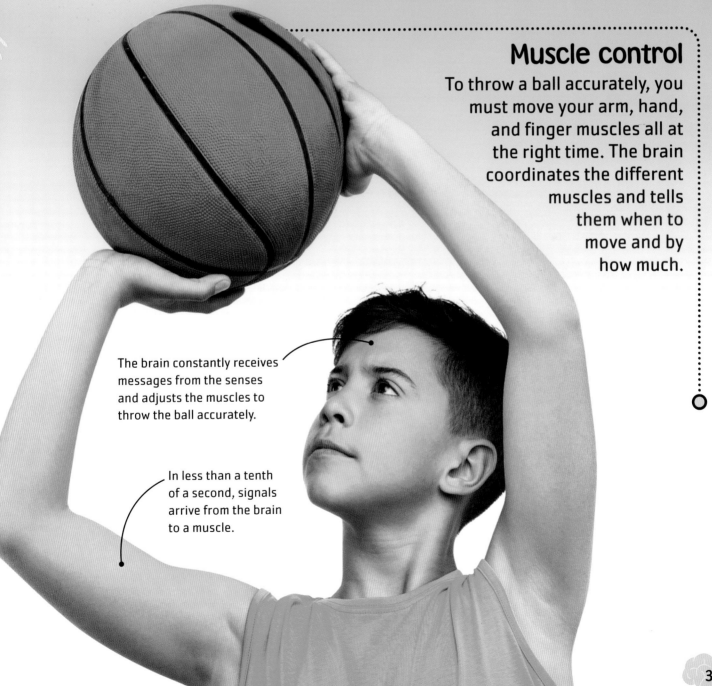

Muscle control

To throw a ball accurately, you must move your arm, hand, and finger muscles all at the right time. The brain coordinates the different muscles and tells them when to move and by how much.

The brain constantly receives messages from the senses and adjusts the muscles to throw the ball accurately.

In less than a tenth of a second, signals arrive from the brain to a muscle.

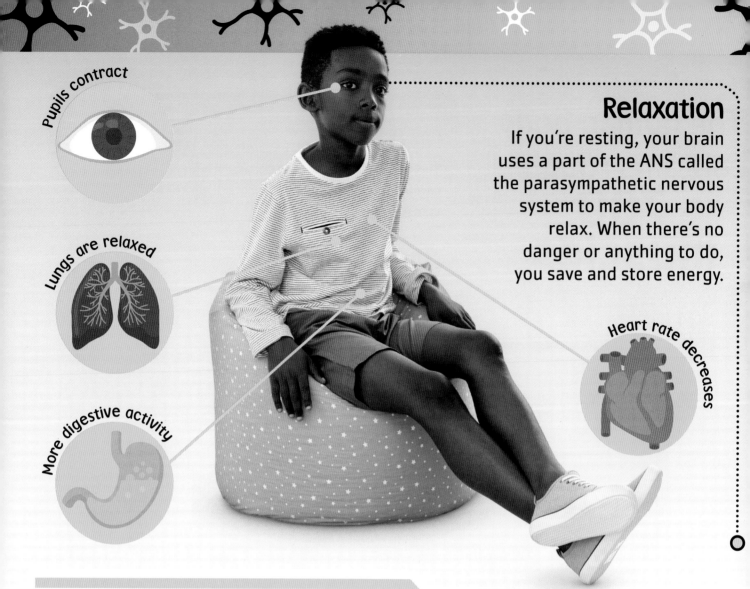

Pupils contract

Lungs are relaxed

More digestive activity

Relaxation

If you're resting, your brain uses a part of the ANS called the parasympathetic nervous system to make your body relax. When there's no danger or anything to do, you save and store energy.

Heart rate decreases

Ready for anything

The brain makes sure the body is ready for what it needs to do— whether that's **relaxation** or **action**. It does this using nerves that run to all parts of the body. These make up the **autonomic nervous system (ANS)**.

VOLUME CONTROL

The more active you are, the more blood your body needs. Your heart always beats, but the ANS can speed it up or slow it down.

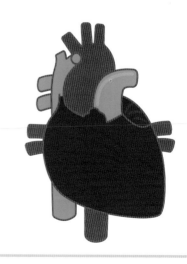

Pupils expand

Lungs are ready

Less digestive activity

Action

When your body needs to get active, your brain uses a different part of the ANS, called the sympathetic nervous system. Digestion is switched off and the rest of the body gets ready to move.

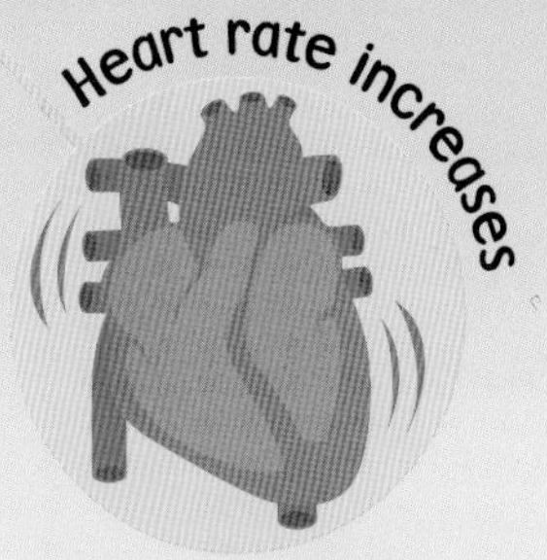

Heart rate increases

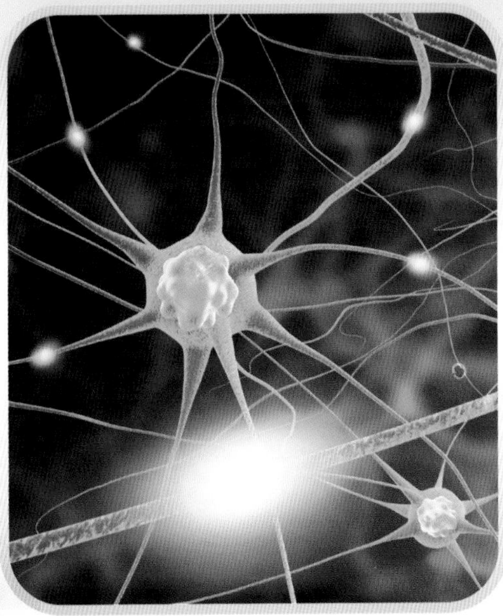

The brain also controls the release of certain chemicals, called hormones, that help prepare the body for action.

Fight or flight?
When a person encounters danger, they need to decide very quickly if they should confront it or run away. The sympathetic nervous system prepares the body to do either.

Knowing what you need!

The brain **knows** when you are too hot or too cold, hungry or full, and what to do about it. Here, we look at how the brain recognizes that you're hungry and **signals** that you should eat.

You absorb the food you have eaten, use up the energy from the food, and start to feel hungry again.

① Feeling hungry

When your stomach is empty, it releases a hormone (chemical messenger) called ghrelin. Ghrelin travels in the blood to the brain, where it sticks to different neurons and makes you feel hungry.

② Hunt for food

When you're hungry, you want food. You might search or ask for it. Your brain helps you to notice anything that smells or looks like food.

4 Feeling full

The intestines below the stomach release hormones that signal food has arrived there. These hormones tell the brain when you have eaten enough, so you feel full and stop eating... for a while.

3 Filling up

When you find food, you eat it! As the stomach fills up, it stops producing ghrelin. Neurons attached to the stomach send messages to the brain, which tell it that the stomach is stretched.

The hypothalamus is the part of the brain that is most important for controlling hunger.

NEGATIVE FEEDBACK

When you are hungry, or full, the brain and body work together to change your behavior, so that you stop feeling that way. Your body and brain use this "negative feedback" to keep you feeling just right.

Baby brains

In the early stages of life, the brain and spinal cord are formed from a structure called the neural tube. The brain grows fast while the baby is in the womb, and it is about the size of a large orange at birth.

3 WEEKS

A neural tube soon develops inside an embryo—the name given to an unborn baby between its second and eighth week.

6 WEEKS

As the embryo grows, the front end of the neural tube grows fastest and divides into different parts.

9 WEEKS

By nine weeks, sections of the neural tube have started to become the spinal cord, hindbrain, midbrain, and forebrain. The unborn baby is now known as a fetus.

Key
- Forebrain
- Midbrain
- Hindbrain
- Spinal cord

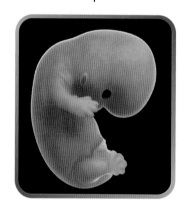

At eight weeks old, a human embryo is the size of a **raspberry**!

Making a **brain**

A human brain forms as a baby grows inside its mother's womb. How it **develops** is controlled by instructions inside the baby's **DNA** and what the baby **senses**.

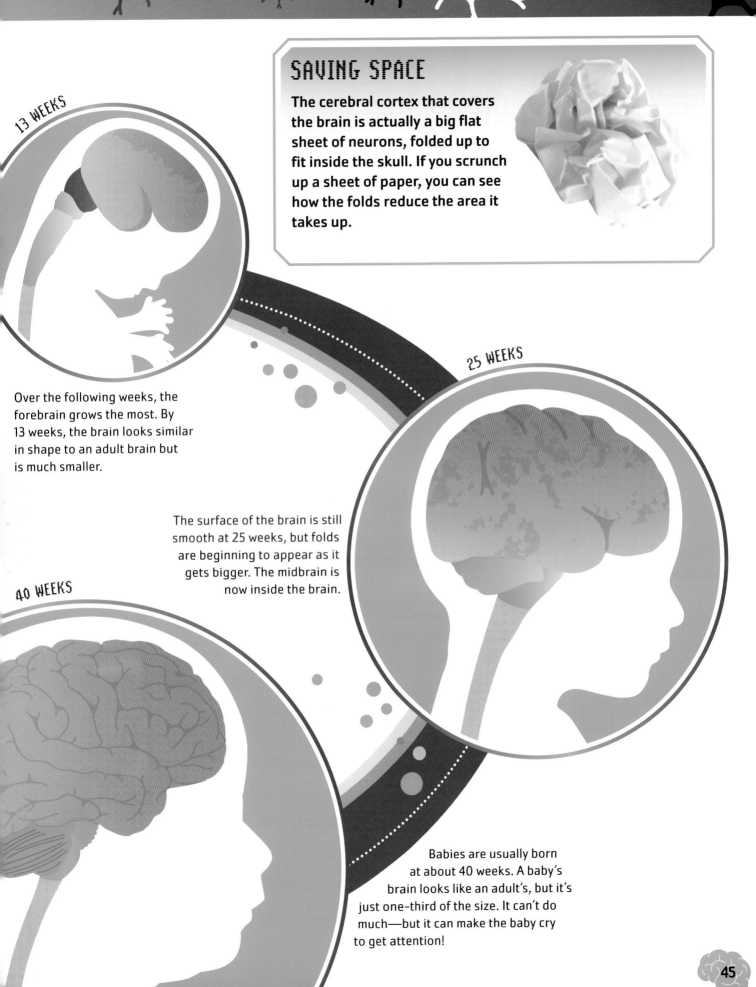

13 WEEKS

SAVING SPACE

The cerebral cortex that covers the brain is actually a big flat sheet of neurons, folded up to fit inside the skull. If you scrunch up a sheet of paper, you can see how the folds reduce the area it takes up.

Over the following weeks, the forebrain grows the most. By 13 weeks, the brain looks similar in shape to an adult brain but is much smaller.

25 WEEKS

The surface of the brain is still smooth at 25 weeks, but folds are beginning to appear as it gets bigger. The midbrain is now inside the brain.

40 WEEKS

Babies are usually born at about 40 weeks. A baby's brain looks like an adult's, but it's just one-third of the size. It can't do much—but it can make the baby cry to get attention!

45

The growing **brain**

When a person is born, their brain still has a lot of **growing** to do. Much of that growing is instructed by **DNA**, but **experiences** also shape how the brain develops.

EXCITING ENVIRONMENTS

Mice that have lots of places and activities to explore grow bigger brains, with more connections between neurons, than mice who live in boring homes. The busier mice are smarter, too!

NEWBORN

TODDLER

TEENAGER

ADULT

Fast, then slow

At birth, the brain is roughly one-third of its adult size. In the first year, it doubles, but then it grows more and more slowly until it is fully grown at about the age of 20.

Wiring the brain

Nearly all the brain's neurons have been made by the time a baby is born. They are, however, very simple, with few connections. Learning and experience shape which synapses form and which are lost.

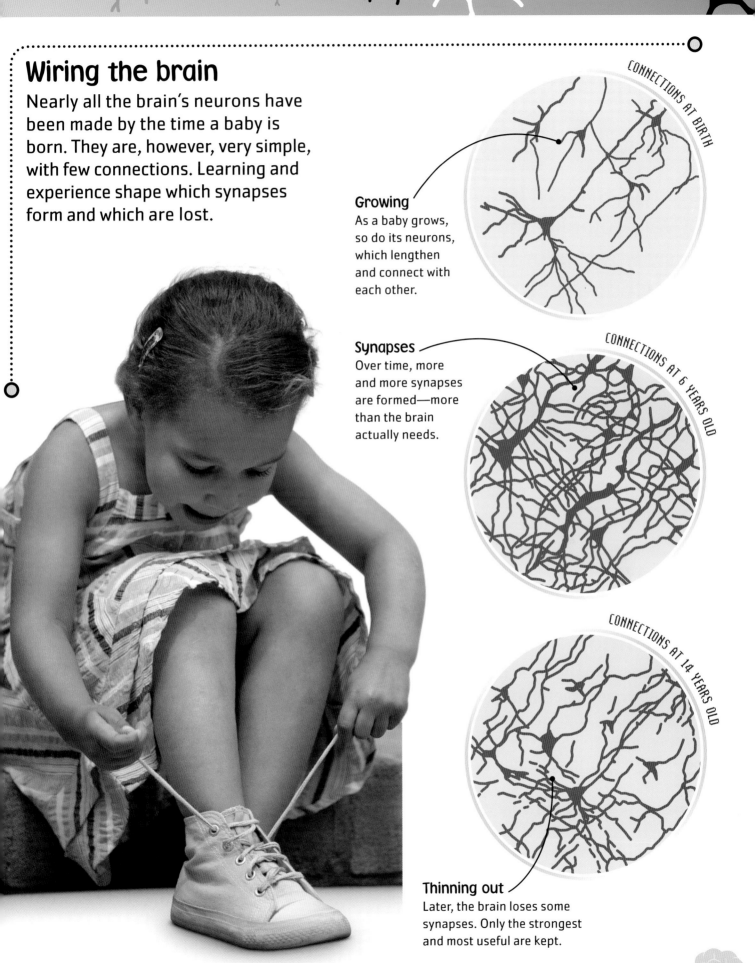

Growing
As a baby grows, so do its neurons, which lengthen and connect with each other.

Synapses
Over time, more and more synapses are formed—more than the brain actually needs.

Thinning out
Later, the brain loses some synapses. Only the strongest and most useful are kept.

How the brain learns

Brains can learn huge amounts of very complicated stuff. The basic way that brains gain **knowledge** is by making **synapses** between neurons that get stronger with **use**!

Brains evolved to have certain instincts built into them from birth. Dog brains know naturally that the smell of meat is the smell of their food—and they like food!

I love learning!

Learning by association

Brains are great at associating, or matching together, different events. If two things happen at the same time that make more than one set of neurons spike, the neurons form strong synapses. Any events can become associated.

Learning by repetition

Why does practicing make us better at something? It's because neurons that repeatedly spike at the same time form stronger synapses. After practice, the memory of what you need to do is recalled much more easily.

If you learn to play the violin, you associate the movements of playing with the notes you play.

BEEP! BEEP! BEEP!

After practice, the synapses that match the movements to the notes become stronger.

BEEP! BEEP! BEEP!

② In contrast, most human-made objects have no strong meaning to animals. They need to learn if they are important. For example, a whistle means nothing to a dog.

③ In a famous experiment, a scientist named Ivan Pavlov asked what happens if every time he fed a dog, the dog heard the same noise.

④ Over time, the dog learned that the sound meant food was coming. The neurons that naturally responded to food became activated by the noise, too.

⑤ By the end of the test, whenever the dog heard the sound, it thought it would be fed. The link was so strong, just hearing the noise made the dog make extra saliva!

Learning by outcome

Brains track what happens whenever you do something. If your actions have good consequences, you learn to repeat those actions. A neurotransmitter called dopamine is released when you do the right thing, which helps make this association stronger.

Dopamine spreads to different areas, such as the hippocampus, where a memory of the good action is recorded.

Dopamine is the reward neurotransmitter.

Making
memories

For the brain to learn things and to **remember** experiences, it needs to make memories. The **hippocampus** in the brain is important for creating memories—but there isn't just one type of **memory**.

At the party
Experiencing or learning something activates a number of neurons in different areas of the cerebral cortex and the hippocampus as the event happens.

Remember when...

I remember that!

Episodic memory creates records of experiences, or "episodes." It's a multistep process that involves a memory forming, being stored, then being recalled. The hippocampus is vital for all of this.

② A memory forms

The spiking of these neurons together strengthens their connections. A memory is stored when the connections between the hippocampus and cerebral cortex get stronger.

③ Can you remember?

Just a small reminder of the event, perhaps what you ate, makes the hippocampus switch those same neurons back on again. Then you remember the whole thing.

OTHER TYPES OF MEMORY

The brain uses different systems to learn new skills or temporarily hold information.

Procedural memory

Learning new skills, or "procedures," like playing the piano, is a different type of memory that doesn't involve the hippocampus. Instead, it requires synapses changing strength in the cerebellum and elsewhere.

Working memory

Holding information in the mind for a short time, such as when you're solving math problems, involves neurons in the cerebral cortex spiking all the time that you're retaining the information.

Emotions

Emotions are your **feelings** about what's happening to you or the world around you. Emotions affect your **body** and **behavior** and how others respond to you.

> You show emotions through facial expressions. These tell others how you're feeling, so they can understand you.

Happy

Sad

Four emotions

Scientists now think there are only four basic emotions: happiness, fear, sadness, and anger. All the many different feelings you have are a mix of these four basic reactions.

Angry

Emotional response

Emotions cause your body and behavior to change—but it works the other way around, too. Your physical state can make you feel a certain way. Take anger, for example:

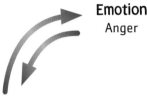

Emotion
Anger

Bodily responses
Fast heartbeat
Deep breaths
Blood goes to muscles ready for action

Behavioral responses
Focus on problem
Shouting
Frowning

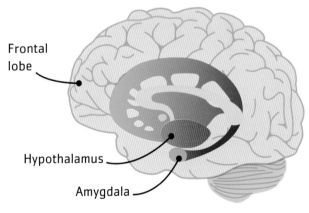

Frontal lobe

Hypothalamus

Amygdala

Where does fear come from?

The amygdala in the center of the brain generates a feeling of fear. The hypothalamus controls your body's response to it, while the frontal lobe shapes how fear affects your behavior.

Scared

Thinking and intelligence

Thinking is the most complex thing a brain does. It involves combining new **sensory information** with previously **stored memories**, figuring out what it all means, then **deciding** what to do.

Remember the worms on page 25? Their simple brains collect sensory information, then automatically respond to it. Sometimes humans do this, but often we stop and think.

Thinking ahead

Intelligence is about solving problems using your imagination. First, you must decide what the goal is, then imagine different actions you could take, and, finally, choose the best option for a happy result. Here's an example:

Oh, no!
Imagine walking along and seeing a friend drop their scarf when it's cold. You can imagine the different outcomes.

Thinking it through
Without the scarf, your friend might get cold. You can also imagine their emotions— they might be sad to have lost it.

Rules vs. creativity

Sometimes intelligence requires figuring out the right answer from known rules—like in math. Other times, the best solution is creating something completely new, like when you write a story or paint a picture.

Finding a solution
If you pick up the scarf and return it to your friend, the problem is solved! They are happy and warm, and you are happy to have helped.

CONSCIOUSNESS

Consciousness is the personal experience of being alive. You aren't conscious when you sleep. The brain's workings create consciousness, but why exactly we feel it is still a great mystery!

Sleeping and dreaming

Every night you do something very mysterious—you **sleep** and **dream**. Scientists don't fully understand why these processes happen, but they do know that they help to keep the brain healthy.

Light and deep sleep

During the night, you move through different types of sleep that have different jobs. In deep sleep, you are very difficult to wake. REM sleep is much lighter, and dreams mainly happen then.

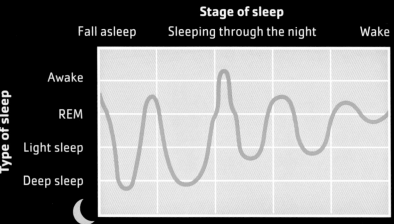

Stage of sleep

Fall asleep   Sleeping through the night   Wake

Type of sleep

Awake
REM
Light sleep
Deep sleep

REM stands for "rapid movement." When you dre your closed eyes dart arou

Daily rhythms

Over each day's 24-hour cycle, your brain and body's activities change to match the time. When it gets dark, the brain tells the body it is time to sleep.

Sorting memories

Scientists think that dreams help mix the new memories you made in the day with memories already stored in your brain. Deep sleep might also help change new memories into long-term ones.

Time to wake up!

Cleaning the brain

When a brain is busy in the day, garbage builds up—including old neurotransmitters and other chemical waste. During deep sleep, the brain washes away this material.

The aging brain

The brain **changes** throughout life—it gets **better** at some things and **worse** at others. Living a **healthy life** can help keep the brain in **good condition**.

Older and wiser

As you get older, you gain more memories and knowledge. Some brain processes keep improving during adulthood, such as certain math skills and thinking about complex problems.

Brain drain

From around 30 years old, human brains start to shrink gradually. Both episodic and working memory get slightly worse with age. Other thought processes also become slower.

Brain illness

Some brain diseases are more common in old age. Alzheimer's disease causes neurons to die and areas of the brain to shrink. This can lead to confusion and forgetfulness.

Healthy brain

Brain with Alzheimer's disease

Cerebral cortex
Thinking can become confused as this area shrinks.

Cerebral cortex
This is where language and thoughts are made and where information is processed.

Hippocampus
This area is essential for the brain to make new memories.

Ventricles
These spaces in the brain get bigger as neurons shrink and die.

Hippocampus
Lots of shrinkage here can cause memory loss and forgetfulness.

HEALTHY BODY, HEALTHY BRAIN

Exercising regularly and eating healthy food helps the brain to age better. It's also important to use your brain a lot—thinking hard and educating yourself may help to protect the brain from illness.

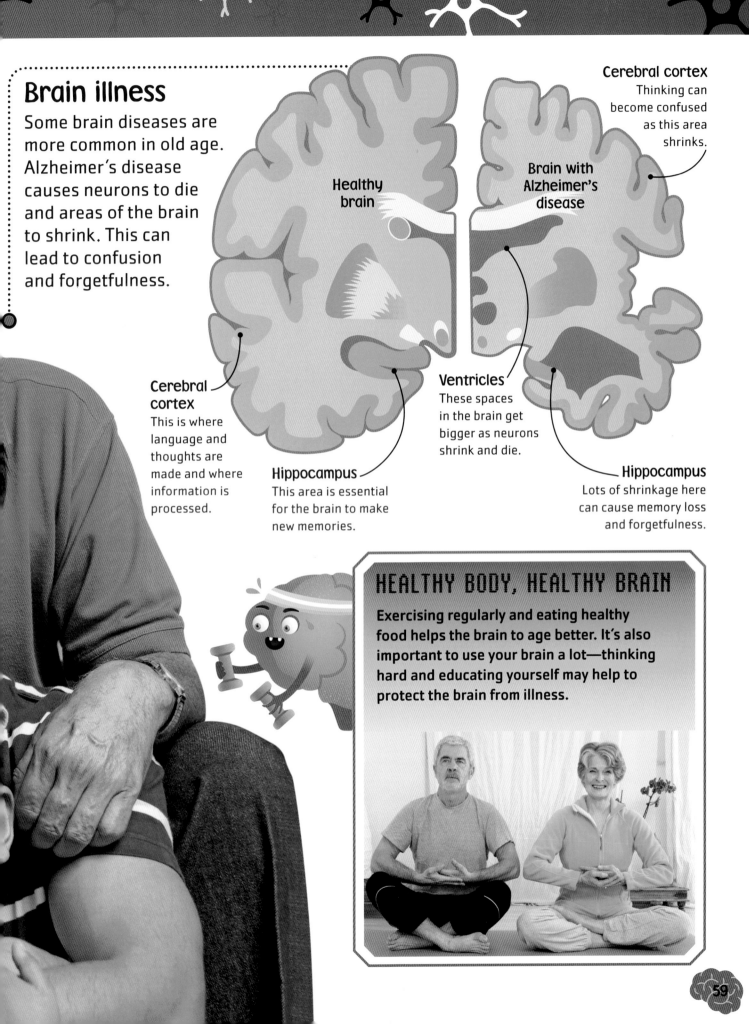

Our different **brains**

A person's DNA and their life experiences shape how their brain works. **Knowing** the differences that can occur in individuals' brains is helpful for **understanding** the challenges some people face.

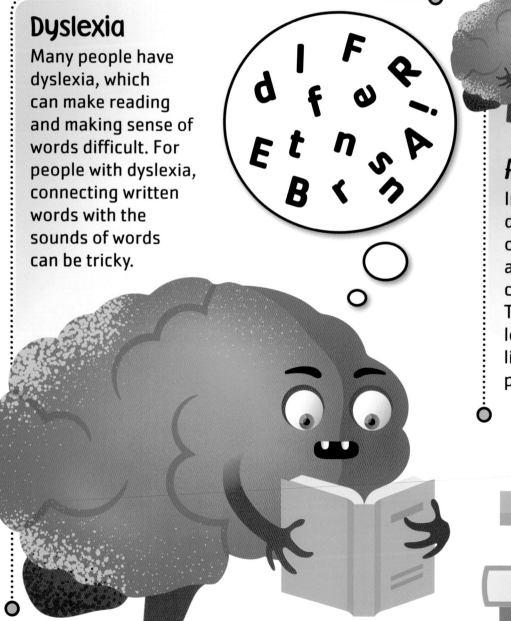

Dyslexia

Many people have dyslexia, which can make reading and making sense of words difficult. For people with dyslexia, connecting written words with the sounds of words can be tricky.

Autism

Individuals can have very different experiences of autism. People with autism often find communication difficult. They may also dislike loud noises and bright lights and find busy places confusing.

MENTAL HEALTH

We can all feel sad and upset from time to time. However, some people feel like this all the time, and this could be a sign that their mental health needs looking after. The reasons can be hard to explain but, just like physical problems, the feelings can be treated and made better.

ADHD

Attention deficit hyperactivity disorder (ADHD) can make it difficult for people to concentrate or to stay still. People with ADHD are often very active and quickly switch from one task to another.

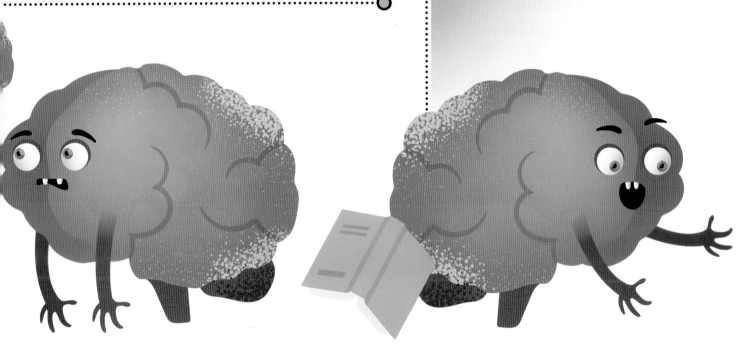

How to help

If you are struggling with a problem, talk to a person you trust. If you see someone else who needs help, ask how they are and always remember to be kind and try to understand their feelings.

» Talk about it. It's good to talk about experiences or changing emotions, to make better sense of them.

» Be kind. Being friendly and kind to someone having a difficult time can make a huge difference.

» Find help. If a problem is making you really worried, ask for help from a trusted adult, such as a parent or teacher.

What's next for
brain science?

Although we know a lot about how the brain works, many **questions** remain. Here are just a few areas still to **explore**.

Consciousness

The hardest problem to understand in neuroscience is why we are conscious. Why are we aware of the workings of our brains? Where does that feeling of being alive come from?

Brain aging

Can we figure out how to stop the brain from slowing down as we get older? Can we prevent the brain diseases associated with old age?

Animal brains

Which animals had the first brains? What are the important differences between different species' brains? What makes humans unique?

Could I be a computer?

Computer brains

Can we make a computer do what brains do? Is it possible to make a conscious computer? Could we one day store our own memories on computers?

Brain diseases

We still don't know exactly what causes most brain diseases. Can we protect people from them? How can we treat these diseases? Can we repair the brain?

Timeline of the brain

Only in recent history have **scientists** begun to understand the **secrets** of the brain and how it works. Every year, scientists still make new **discoveries** about this amazing organ.

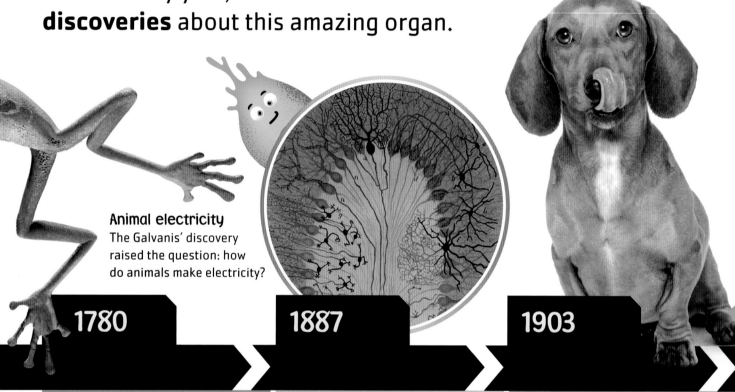

Animal electricity
The Galvanis' discovery raised the question: how do animals make electricity?

1780

1887

1903

Electric animals

Luigi and **Lucia Galvani** conduct experiments on frogs. They discover that when a **spark** of electricity touches a dead frog's leg, it makes it twitch. This suggests that **nerves** move muscles by carrying **electrical signals**.

Drawing the neuron

Santiago Ramón y Cajal is the first person to accurately describe the structure of **nerve cells**, or neurons. He uses **microscopes and dyes** to show that brains are made up of many types of neuron and creates beautiful drawings of them.

Dribbling dogs

Ivan Pavlov trains dogs to **associate** a particular sound, such as a buzzer, with **being fed**. He notes that after this training, their mouths start to produce saliva in response to the sound alone. This becomes known as "**classical conditioning**."

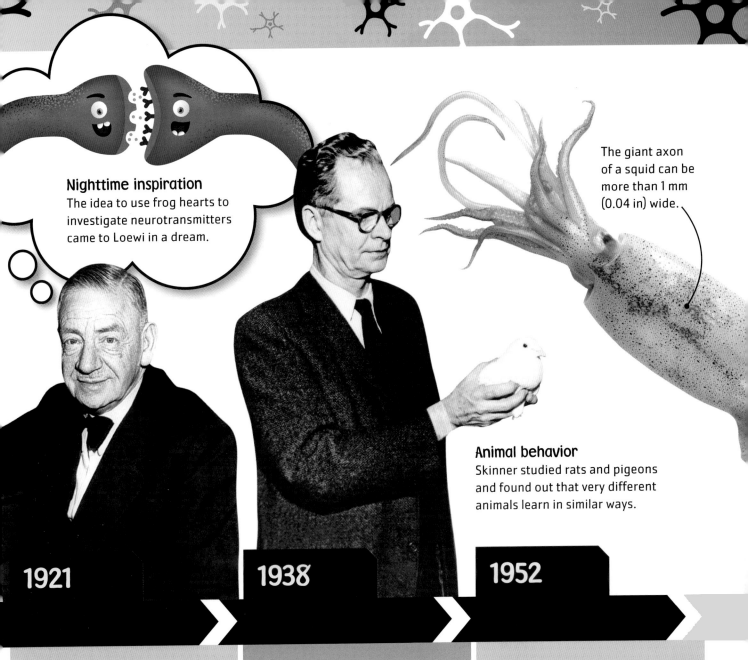

Nighttime inspiration
The idea to use frog hearts to investigate neurotransmitters came to Loewi in a dream.

The giant axon of a squid can be more than 1 mm (0.04 in) wide.

Animal behavior
Skinner studied rats and pigeons and found out that very different animals learn in similar ways.

1921

1938

1952

Chemical messengers

Otto Loewi discovers the chemical messengers **neurotransmitters** by electrically zapping the nerve to a frog's heart and collecting the **chemicals** this releases. He gives the chemicals to a second frog heart and they **change** how fast the heart beats.

Rewarding good behavior

Burrhus Frederic Skinner describes how animals learn to repeat behaviors that are **rewarded**, such as when they receive a treat, and stop doing ones that are punished. He calls this **"operant learning."**

Electrical spikes

Alan Hodgkin and **Andrew Huxley** show how nerve cells make **electrical spikes** by measuring electricity in the **giant axons** of squid.

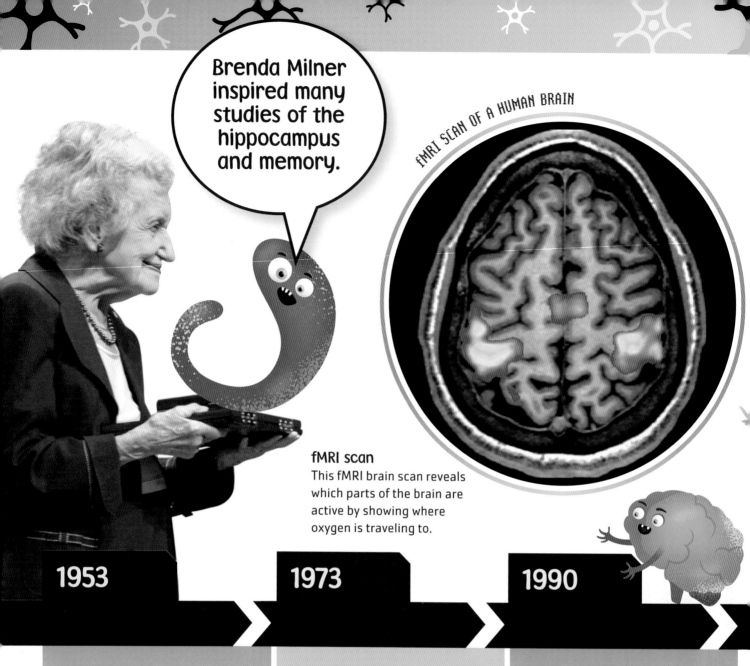

Brenda Milner inspired many studies of the hippocampus and memory.

fMRI scan
This fMRI brain scan reveals which parts of the brain are active by showing where oxygen is traveling to.

1953

1973

1990

No new memories

Neuroscientist **Brenda Milner** reports a case study of a man who is unable to form new memories after losing the **hippocampus** from both sides of his brain.

Changing synapses

Tim Bliss and **Terje Lømo** show that when synapses are activated repeatedly, they become stronger. This helps to show how we **learn** and how **memories** are formed and stored in the brain.

ACTIVE SYNAPSE

Looking inside

Seiji Ogawa discovers a way to watch the oxygen in blood move around the brain. Known as **functional magnetic resonance imaging** (fMRI), the technology can be used to see which parts of the brain are **active** during different activities.

In **2019**, scientists published almost **100,000** new **studies** on the brain!

Hello!

Apple

Hello!

2005

2012

2019

Lighting the way

Karl Deisseroth and his colleagues put a light-sensitive protein—normally found in **algae**—into neurons. It makes neurons **spike** when light shines on them, which enables new **experiments** where specific neurons can be activated.

Clever computer

Alex Krizhevsky, Ilya Sutskever and **Geoff Hinton** design a computer program called AlexNet. Inspired by **neurons**, the program is better than a human at **recognizing** photographs of certain objects.

Decoding speech

From looking only at neuron **spikes** in the brain, **Gopala Anumanchipalli, Josh Chartier**, and **Edward Chang** use a computer to figure out what a person is saying—even if the person only pretends to say the words.

Glossary

These words are helpful to know when talking and learning about the brain.

amygdala
small grape-shaped brain region important for feeling emotions, especially fear

autonomic nervous system (ANS)
group of nerves that connect the brain with the body's organs and blood vessels

axon
thin, wirelike structure extending from a neuron along which electrical messages travel

brain
organ that is the main part of the nervous system. It receives sensory input, processes and stores information, and controls the body's movements

brain stem
region at the base of the brain controlling essential functions, such as heart rate and breathing

case study
investigation into a single person to whom something medically unusual has happened

cell
basic building block of all life forms

central nervous system (CNS)
brain and spinal cord combined

cerebellum
region at the back of the brain important for coordinating movement and balance

cerebral cortex
outer layer of the brain, important for many complex brain functions. It is divided into four lobes

circadian rhythm
changes in behavior or bodily functions that happen at particular times of day

consciousness
feeling of being aware of your own thoughts and experiences

cortex
short for cerebral cortex, or one part of the cerebral cortex that controls a particular function, such as the visual cortex

cranium
part of the skull that contains the brain

dendrite
branch of a neuron that receives incoming signals from synapses

dopamine
neurotransmitter important for movement and learning

emotion
strong feeling, usually associated with what's happening to you

fMRI (functional magnetic resonance imaging)
brain scan that shows the oxygen in blood in the brain

forebrain
large region of the brain that includes the cerebral cortex

ganglion
small cluster of neurons

gray matter
regions of the CNS that appear gray because the neurons don't have much myelin

hindbrain
region of the brain that includes the cerebellum and brain stem

hippocampus
long, thin brain structure essential for memory formation

hormone
chemical messenger released into the blood

hypothalamus
structure in the brain important for controlling bodily functions

impulse
brief spike of electrical activity, also called a spike or action potential

instinct
built-in reaction to a certain situation that isn't learned

limbic system
group of brain structures having to do with emotions and memory, including the amygdala, hypothalamus, and hippocampus

lobe
one of the four large regions of the cerebral cortex consisting of the occipital, frontal, parietal, and temporal lobe

medulla
bottom part of the brain stem

memory
record of an event, fact, or action stored in the brain. The hippocampus is important in the process of storing and retrieving memories

midbrain
region in the center of the brain that controls many basic functions

MRI (magnetic resonance imaging)
brain scan that shows the structure of the brain

muscle
organ that can shorten or lengthen to make the body move

myelin
fatty substance made by oligodendrocytes that surrounds the axons of some neurons

myelin sheath
sleeve of myelin around an axon that makes spikes travel faster

negative feedback
system that stops something from happening to an extreme. When a feeling, such as hunger or fullness, starts increasing, the brain activates systems that stop it

nerve
bundle of axons running from one place to another

neuron
cell that creates electrical signals and releases neurotransmitters to pass messages through the nervous system

neuroscientist
person who studies the brain or nervous system

neurotransmitter
chemical released by neurons to signal to other neurons or cells

organ
group of cells that work together to do a job, such as the heart, eye, or brain

parasympathetic nervous system
part of the ANS that relaxes the body

pathway
connection between two brain regions created by neurons

peripheral nervous system
all neurons outside of the CNS

pons
part of the brain stem with multiple functions, including breathing, sensing, and feeling pain

receptor
tiny structure on a cell that detects sensory information, such as light and touch, or neurotransmitters

reflex
automatic response to a certain event that is not consciously controlled; for example, sneezing

REM (rapid eye movement)
type of sleep state associated with dreaming

skull
collection of bones in the head

sleep
brain state in which consciousness is lost and dreaming happens

spike
brief increase of electrical activity, also called an impulse or action potential

spinal cord
part of the CNS that runs inside the spine and carries and processes information between the brain and body

spine
backbone. The bones that contain the spinal cord

sympathetic nervous system
part of the ANS that prepares the body for action

synapse
junction between two neurons across which neurotransmitters travel

thalamus
brain structure important for relaying sensory information from sense organs to the cerebral cortex

ventricle
fluid-filled space within the brain

white matter
regions of the CNS that appear white because the neurons have lots of myelin

Index

Ii

imagination 54
information processing 9, 11, 24–25
inhibitory synapses 23
intelligence 54–55
iris 34

Kk

knowledge 48–49, 58

Ll

language 11, 59
learning 47, 48–49, 50, 64, 65, 66
lens 34
light 34–35, 67
limbic system 10, 14
lobes 10–11
lungs 40–41

Mm

memory 6, 9, 10, 13, 14, 32, 50–51, 54, 57, 58, 59, 66
mental health 61
mice 46
microglia 19
microscopes 13, 64
movement 6, 8–9, 10, 25, 38–39, 41
MRI scanners 12–13
muscles 8, 24, 38–39, 53
myelin sheath 18, 19, 21

Nn

negative feedback 43
nervous system 7, 25, 40–41
neural tube 44
neurons 13, 15, 17, 18–23, 30–37, 45, 47, 59, 64, 67
neuroscience 12–13, 14, 25, 62–67
neurotransmitters 22, 49, 57, 65
nose 32
nucleus 17

Oo

occipital lobe 11
octopuses 26–27
oligodendrocytes 19
operant learning 65
optic nerve 35
optical illusions 35
outcome, learning by 49
oxygen 13, 16, 66

Pp

pain 8, 30
parasympathetic nervous system 40
parietal lobe 11
pericytes 19
peripheral nervous system 7
plants 25
practice 48
pressure 11, 30, 31
problem-solving 10, 54–55, 58
procedural memory 51
pupil 34, 40–41

Rr

reading 11, 60
receptors 30, 32, 33, 34, 35, 36, 37
reflexes 24–25
relaxation 40
REM sleep 56
repairs 19
repetition, learning by 48
retina 35
rewards 49, 65
rules, following 55

Ss

sadness 52
sea squirts 27
senses 7, 8–9, 20, 24–25, 30–37, 39, 44, 54
shrews 27

sight 8, 11, 13, 34–35

sight 8, 11, 13, 34–35
skills 48, 51, 58
skin 30–31
skull 28–29
sleep 8, 55, 56–57
smell 10, 32–33
sneezing 24
sound 36–37
speech 9, 10, 67
spiders 27
spikes 15, 20–23, 24, 31, 48, 51, 65, 67
spinal cord 6, 24, 31, 44–45
squid 65
stirrup bone 36
stomach 40–41, 42–43
swallowing 11
sympathetic nervous system 41
synapses 15, 19, 20–23, 47, 48, 51, 66

Tt

taste 11, 32–33
temperature 30, 42
temporal lobe 11
thalamus 35
thinking 6, 9, 20, 25, 54–55, 59
thirst 8, 10
tongue 32–33
touch 11, 30–31
triceps 38

Vv

ventricles 59
Venus flytraps 25
vibrations 36, 37
visual cortex 35

Ww

white matter 21
working memory 51, 58
worms 25, 54

Acknowledgments

DK would like to thank: Jolyon Goddard, Katie Lawrence, Kathleen Teece, and Seeta Parmar for editorial assistance; Arran Lewis for CGI illustration; Caroline Hunt for proofreading; Helen Peters for compiling the index; and Dr. Victoria Uwannah for consulting on "Our different brains."

The author would like to dedicate this book to Isabella and Mariana: "May your brilliant brains forever thrive."

The publisher would like to thank the following for their kind permission to reproduce their photographs:

(Key: a-above; b-below/bottom; c-center; f-far; l-left; r-right; t-top)

4-5 Dreamstime.com: Matthieuclouis. **6 Dreamstime.com**: MNStudio (bl). **8-9 Dreamstime.com:** Wavebreakmedia Ltd (c). **12 Alamy Stock Photo:** B pics / Stockimo (br). **Dreamstime.com:** Tyler Olson (cl). Science Photo Library: Living Art Enterprises (tr). **13 Dreamstime.com:** Dgm007 / Dmitriy Melnikov (cb); Gekaskr (cra); Stradnic Stanislav (cr). Science Photo Library: Steve Gschmeissner (clb); Living Art Enterprises (tl). **14 Dreamstime.com:** Sebastian Kaulitzki (ca, cra). Getty Images / iStock: SciePro (cl). **15 123RF.com:** Kateryna Kon (crb). Science Photo Library: Jose Calvo (tl). **16 Dreamstime.com:** Mercedes Maldonado (bl). **16-17 Science Photo Library:** Ralph Hutchings, Visuals Unlimited. **17 Dreamstime.com:** Ldarin (cr). **20-21 123RF.com:** epicstockmedia. **23 Alamy Stock Photo:** RZUS_Images (tr). **24 Dreamstime.com:** Olgagorovenko (bl). **24-25 Science Photo Library**: Wim Van Egmond (c). **25 123RF.com:** Heiti Paves (cr).

Dreamstime.com: Nico99 (bc). **26-27 Getty Images:** Reynold Mainse / Design Pics. **27 Alamy Stock Photo:** cbimages (crb); Mike Lane (cra). naturepl.com: Ingo Arndt (cr). **29 naturepl.com:** Anup Shah (crb). **30 Dreamstime.com:** Nynke Van Holten (bl). **32 Dreamstime.com:** Sorayut (tr). **34 Shutterstock.com:** wavebreakmedia (cl). **35 123RF.com:** Yurii Perepadia (br). **36 Science Photo Library:** Steve Gschmeissner (tr). **39 Dreamstime.com:** Maxim Lupascu (b). **41 Getty Images / iStock:** cosmin4000 (crb); shapecharge (c). **42-43 Getty Images / iStock:** chuckcollier (c). **43 Dreamstime.com:** Denismart (bc). **44 Alamy Stock Photo:** Science Photo Library / SCIEPRO (cb). **46 Alamy Stock Photo:** Juniors Bildarchiv GmbH / F314 (bl). **47 Alamy Stock Photo:** Picture Partners (bl). **50-51 Dreamstime.com:** Robert Kneschke. **51 Alamy Stock Photo:** Tetra Images, LLC / JGI / Tom Grill (crb). **Dreamstime.com:** Ian Allenden (cra). **52 Getty Images / iStock:** E+ / baona (br). **53 Dreamstime.com:** Esther19775 (bl); Jure Gasparic (tl). **55 Dreamstime.com:** Odua (tl). **56-57 Dreamstime.com:** Wavebreakmedia Ltd (b). **58-59 Alamy Stock Photo**: Indiapicture / Hemant Mehta (c). **59 Alamy Stock Photo:**

fStop Images GmbH / Andreas Stamm (br). **60-61 123RF.com:** Nadezhda Prokudina (tc). **61 Dreamstime.com:** Kmitu (b). **62-63 Dreamstime.com**: Ilexx (bc). **Science Photo Library**: Sinclair Stammers (tc). **62 Dreamstime.com:** Leo Lintang (cra); Wave Break Media Ltd (clb). **63 Dreamstime.com:** Newbi1 (crb). **Getty Images / iStock:** wigglestick (cra). **64 Alamy Stock Photo:** Album (ca). **Dreamstime.com:** Damedeeso (cra). **65 Alamy Stock Photo:** Pictorial Press Ltd (cla); Science History Images (ca). **Fotolia:** Karl Bolf (cra). **66 Dreamstime.com:** Spectral-design (bc). **Getty Images:** AFP / Torstein Boe (tl). **Science Photo Library**: Living Art Enterprises (tr). **67 Dorling Kindersley:** Natural History Museum, London (cl). Dreamstime.com: Andreaobzerova (tr); Orcea David / Orcearo (c, cr). **Fotolia:** Matthew Cole (tl)

Cover images: *Front:* Dreamstime.com: Sebastian Kaulitzki crb, Sebastian Kaulitzki / Eraxion clb; *Back:* Dreamstime.com: Whitehoune clb; PunchStock: tl

All other images © Dorling Kindersley

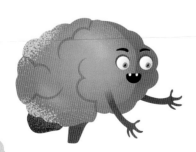